Successful Parenthood

Successful Parenthood

How to Teach Your Child Values, Competence, and Responsibility

Wesley C. Becker

Janis W. Becker

 FOLLETT PUBLISHING COMPANY
Chicago

To Helen and Beck

Second Printing

Library of Congress Catalog Card Number: 73–91582

ISBN 0–695–80448–0

Contents

Preface

Successful Parenthood has been written to help parents learn to be more effective with their children. Our goal is to show parents how to systematically use sound learning principles to teach children in positive ways what they need to learn to become effective people. Technical language has been kept to a minimum and examples are used to illustrate the main points.

One of the most frequent comments received from parents who have used earlier versions of this book is, "Why didn't someone teach me that ten years ago?" Another common comment is, "My whole attitude about punishment has changed. I now know how to work positively with my child. It's better for all of us."

The information in this book can change your life by helping you become a more active participant in the process of rearing your children.

There is a great deal of confusion among parents and writers who provide information for parents about the use of knowledge from the scientific study of human behavior. Many readers of this book may be turned off by the very idea of trying to use learning principles to teach their children to be better human beings. To help those for whom this may be a problem we have discussed many of the issues in case-study form. The first chapter deals with some common misunderstandings about applications of behavioral psychology. If you have questions and doubts, reserve judgment until you have read Chapter One.

1 | *Who Really Cares?*

Adults who take a scientifically-based approach to the care of children are often attacked for *not caring* about children by those who call themselves "child-oriented," or "humanistically-oriented." An attitude exists that to use scientific knowledge is incompatible with being a "good" human being. It can be argued, however, that *effective* care and caring can only exist when parents know ahead of time how their actions will effect their children; that is, when parents know enough about the learning process to anticipate the effects of their behavior on their children. Consider the following case study.

AN INFANT TYRANT

Jimmy is the nineteen-month-old son of Doug and Linda. During dinner, Jimmy repeatedly threw his spoon off his tray, grabbed food from his mother's plate, and yelled in protest if he was stopped while taking food. His loving parents followed these actions by picking up the spoon and giving it back to him and giving him more food. It was quite clear that neither parent was pleased that Jimmy did these things. In fact they got angry at him several times during dinner. And yet nearly all of their reactions to Jimmy's misbehaviors were events that were likely to strengthen Jimmy's misbehavior, such as when he threw a spoon and the action was followed by getting the spoon back and food. His parents were teaching him behaviors that they would later have to punish him for. Jimmy's loving parents were responsible for teaching him behaviors that led them to get angry at him.

Later that night when Jimmy was put to bed, he threw his bottle out of the crib and yelled "Baba," "baba," loudly until his mother retrieved it for him. Linda would go in, pick up the bottle, give Jimmy a hug and some soft words, and settle him down again. It should come as no surprise that this kind of happening became a nightly event lasting nearly an hour. It disturbed the precious time of the day when his parents wanted a few minutes with each other. Again, Jimmy's parents were responsible for what he learned.

We are all products of our learning histories. How we behave, what we think, and the language we speak has been taught to us by our environment and the people in it. A key principle governing our learning is that behaviors that are rewarded will occur more often, and behaviors that are not rewarded or are punished, will occur less often. Much of this book is simply a refinement, elaboration, and application of this principle.

If Linda and Doug knew the principles covered in this book, they could become more responsible parents who could teach Jimmy to be a more lovable child and a more loving child. For example, at mealtime Linda and Doug could give Jimmy more attention when he eats properly with his spoon, rather than waiting for him to misbehave before attending to him. The food given to Jimmy could be more carefully selected as food he likes. When the spoon was thrown on the floor, they could have left it there for awhile, instead of running to get it. And they could stop giving him food from their plates and attention immediately after he misbehaved. They could focus on rewarding more grown-up eating habits and not rewarding his "baby" behavior.

The solution to the bedtime problem requires that his parents no longer go to Jimmy and retrieve his bottle. Doug and Linda could get Jimmy ready for bed with a story, love, and milk; and then tell him he will not get his bottle back if he throws it out. The first night Jimmy might cry a lot, but by the third night, if handled consistently, Jimmy should be going right off to sleep without much fussing. The gain would be a more comfortable evening for everyone.

Who Cares?

Being loving and giving is not enough by itself to insure that we do our best to help those we love. Linda and Doug loved Jimmy, but they were unaware that they were teaching him to do many things they did not like. To be responsible, to contribute to a better future for others, we must *know enough about our effects on others* to determine whether our kindness is really helpful in the long run or not. If you really care, take time to learn about the causes of behavior and use this knowledge in a responsible way.

Other Issues

Two other issues, in addition to that of caring, arise when the systematic use of knowledge of learning enters a discussion. These are the control issue and the bribery issue.

The control issue is this: If the principles of behavioral psychology can be used to predict the outcomes of our actions with others, we can use this knowledge to control others. As a matter of fact, effective parents do control the development of their children, and effective teachers do control what is learned by students. Throughout all history people have been teaching (controlling the learning of) other people. There is no other way except to abdicate all responsibility for others. The main confusion arises (and emotion rises) when the predictable learning outcomes we call teaching get confused with *control by force*. As you will see, we rarely recommend that parents control their children by force; we recommend teaching through the use of positive consequences (teaching with love). Tyrants could use force to control others, and they have. But parents and people in general do not have to be tyrants. The principles of learning do permit us to teach others more effectively along directions we value, but they do not make us value actions and outcomes we would not otherwise value.

Throughout history, man has been controlled by his environment. We have been taught by the consequences of our behavior to avoid the freezing cold or to seek the warmth of the sun. Over time, however, as B. F. Skinner has eloquently pointed out, man has learned to control the environment that controls him. For some time people have been engineering new physical environments that are kinder to them, more rewarding, and less punishing. There have been some goofs, like pollution, but the degree of control man now exercises over this physical environment is remarkable.

People have also become more thoughtful about engineering the social environment in which they live. Political systems and family systems can be seen to be changing from control by force to control by reason and positive consequences. The important point here is that *if we are all products of our learning history,* and the interactions with others are part of that history, then we are truly our brothers' keepers. We are each responsible for how those around us behave with us. We teach them how to behave toward us by how we behave with them. With knowledge of behavior principles we can build better people and be happier ourselves, just as with knowledge of physical principles we can build better physical environments. At the least today, right now, you can become a more effective parent.

The bribery issue arose through the teachings of psychologists in the 1930s. There is no question that bribery is not a good practice. But many parents have mistaken this recommendation to mean that one never uses rewards such as candy or money to motivate children to learn new skills. The recommendation arose because many parents misused rewards. For example, Johnny does not do his assigned chores, so mother says, "I'll give you ten cents if you'll do them right now." That is bribery: it teaches Johnny *not* to do his chores so that his mother will up the ante. That is not the way to use consequences, nor is it desirable to teach children to use parents in this way. When rewards are used to motivate a slow learner or to teach children to be responsible, they are used more in the way adults contract with each other. "If you carry out your responsibilities, these good consequences will happen. If you choose not to carry out your responsibilities, you lose the good consequences." You get paid if you work, not for goofing off. When rewards are used in this way, they are used to strengthen desired behaviors rather than undesired behaviors. Keep in mind that positive consequences in one form or another are important to all of us as adults. Few of us work for no pay or just for the love of work. Why shouldn't positive consequences also be important to children? They are. Learn to use them effectively through the pages that follow.

2 | *Consequences Count*

Danny was a six-year-old boy who was brought to a child clinic because of parents who could not stand his bossy and demanding behavior. Danny determined when he went to bed, when he got fed, what he would eat, and even when his parents would play with him. His parents met his demands, although they did not like them. When occasionally they would refuse to meet his demands, Danny would begin to shout and cry and his parents would give in.

At the clinic, Danny's mother was instructed to interact with him in a playroom just as she would at home. Observers then developed a system for recording how frequently Danny gave his mother commands and how frequently he was cooperative. Commands were statements like "Now we'll play this" or "No, that's wrong. Do it this way." During initial observation procedures, Danny gave his mother commands about four times a minute. Mother was then instructed not to respond to Danny's commands, but to respond to Danny when he showed cooperative behavior (nonimperative statements, actions or questions). To help mother learn to do this, a light was turned on to tell her to respond when Danny showed cooperative behavior. Before too long she could tell the difference on her own. Danny's commanding behavior dropped to zero after two twenty-minute sessions, and his cooperative behaviors rose to about three a minute. To be sure that it was a change in mother's behavior that was responsible for the change in Danny, mother was asked to go back to responding to commands. When she did this, Danny's commanding behavior returned. This convinced mother of her role in supporting Danny's commanding behavior, and she returned to giving attention to cooperative behavior.

Danny's mother was now ready to take what she had learned about the effects of her behavior in teaching Danny to be bossy and use this new knowledge to teach Danny to be more cooperative at home.[1]

AGGRESSIVE ROREY LEARNS TO BEHAVE

Rorey was four years and eight months old. He was an only child of average intelligence. He was brought to an experimental preschool because he could not get along in two other preschools. He showed many objectionable behaviors such as fighting, screaming, disobedience, and bossing. In his new preschool, over several months, his objectionable behaviors had declined to an acceptable level, but he was still a problem at home.

Home observations were begun to see what was going on and to help mother improve his behavior. At home it was obvious that Rorey was well-developed and physically active. He screamed in playing with peers, bossed other children, and enforced his demands with punches and kicks. Observation of mother's behavior indicated that she often gave excessive attention to Rorey's misbehavior and was not consistent in her attempts to discipline him.

Rorey's behavior was recorded for an hour a day. During initial observation periods, Rorey was found to follow only

30 percent of the instructions given to him by his mother. He showed aggressive acts in 10 percent of the twenty-second observation intervals used to record his behavior. Yelling occurred in 25 percent of the observation intervals and bossing in 14 percent.

Rorey's mother was then given instructions (and assistance in following them) designed to change Rorey's behavior. Immediately after Rorey showed aggression or disobedience he was to be sent to a bedroom alone (without toys). Mother was to say to him when he was aggressive, "You cannot stay here if you fight." If he was disobedient, mother was to say, "You cannot stay here if you do not do what you are told." After these comments (and no others), Rorey was sent to the bedroom and required to stay there alone until he was quiet (no tantrums or cries) for two minutes. When it was time to come out, mother was to open the door and let him return to his regular activities without further comment. Mother was also instructed not to respond to other misbehavior (she was to ignore behavior not meriting punishment) and to reinforce cooperative play with praise and attention (at least once every five minutes). Special treats, such as a new toy, a cold drink, or a cookie, could be used to reward Rorey when he obeyed or showed desirable play.

When the consequences for behavior were changed, so did Rorey's behavior. Under this new system, Rorey followed mother's instructions 78 percent of the time. Aggressive behavior and yelling dropped to near zero and bossing was cut in half. Mother and Rorey had developed more positive ways of interacting.[2]

CONSEQUENCES STRENGTHEN OR WEAKEN BEHAVIOR

The rapid changes in Danny and Rorey were both brought about through the use of these basic principles of behavior change:

Principle 1: To increase the rate of some behavior (accelerate how often it happens), *follow the behavior* with rewards or good consequences.

Principle 2: To decrease the rate of some behavior (decelerate how often it happens), *follow the behavior* with a punishing consequence.

Principle 3: It is also possible to weaken behavior by *no longer following the behavior* with rewards or good consequences. (This procedure is called extinction. When extinction is used to weaken behavior, you should first expect the behavior to "get a little worse before it gets better.")

In the case of Danny, his cooperative behavior was reinforced by attention and verbal responses from mother. Danny's commanding behavior was placed on extinction by mother no longer giving in to his demands.

Rorey's behavior was changed by using all three basic change principles. Rorey's aggressive and disobedient behavior was weakened by punishment (placing him alone in his room). Withdrawing reinforcers is very often a better punishment procedure than hurting a child. As we shall see in Chapter Five, punishment by withholding opportunity for reinforcement can be very effective. Rorey's mother also reinforced cooperative behavior and obedience with attention, praise, and goodies. Finally, she placed other undesired behavior on extinction by ignoring them. She no longer followed them with excessive attention.

There is one additional principle important to the effective use of consequences:

Principle 4: It is necessary to *test out* any particular consequence to be sure it is a reinforcer or punisher for a particular child.

Rorey's mother thought that scolding him and showing her concern when he misbehaved would punish his misbehavior. But scolding had just the opposite effect. Mother's attention appeared to function to strengthen Rorey's misbehavior. A lot of problem behavior has just this basis. Parents must be on guard to carefully examine their assumptions and the effects of their behavior on their children. *The basic rule is to find out what works.*

Many consequences that influence what we do are a natural part of our everyday environment. We avoid extreme cold and extreme heat. We plant and harvest foods so that we can eat them. We walk carefully so as not to fall, to bump something, or to get run over by a truck. Today, the environmental consequences that influence our behavior are more and more from a man-made environment—buildings, air conditioners, food storage systems, heaters, and the like, which protect us from extreme physical discomfort. If we look at our physical and social environment in terms of the critical consequences that influence our behavior, we can immediately increase our power to effectively deal with problems. We become more aware of what needs to be done to help others learn to be better people. We become more aware of what may be critical and not critical in the design of our personal environments.

Consequences determine what is learned. This book is designed to help you learn to use consequences to teach your child *what you want him to learn.* As you will see, you first need to find out what consequences are effective with your child. Then you need to learn how to use the consequences to strengthen desired responses and weaken undesired responses.

For the remainder of this chapter and in the next two chapters we will not talk about punishment. If you are eager to try out some newly learned ideas, we suggest you not include the use of punishment in your experimenting until you have completed the more thorough treatment of the issues surrounding punishment as presented in Chapter Five.

Our next task is to learn more about positive consequences —how to identify and create them.

NATURAL AND LEARNED REINFORCERS

Some reinforcers are effective for most people because of the way we are built. The natural reinforcers, which "come with the baby," include such things as food, water, warmth, tactile stimulation, and activity. Some of the more important reinforcers in the lives of people are, however, learned. We learn to respond to attention from others. We learn to work for status and prestige. We learn to value money and trading stamps. We learn to work for grades and teacher praise. Because some reinforcers can be learned, or *fail to be learned,* it is important for parents to know how to teach their children to be responsive to the kinds of learned reinforcers that our society depends upon.

The basic procedure to use to create a new reinforcer is this:

Principle 5: To make a reinforcing stimulus out of a neutral stimulus, repeatedly follow the neutral stimulus with a known reinforcer.

For the young infant, mother's voice and physical presence are quite neutral. The infant might startle at the sound of a voice, but mother's voice and presence have little effect in quieting crying and the like. With repeated situations, however, where mother's voice and physical presence are followed by being held, rocked, fed, and other activities that relieve discomfort, mother's voice and presence (attention) become learned reinforcers. A hungry baby will quiet just because mother came into the room or said some soft words. In like fashion, praise words from parents, such as "That's really good," or "Nice job," will become reinforcers for most children if the praise words are at first closely followed by other "good things," such as a cookie, a warm hug, a special privilege, or fun things to do. When children have learned to respond to attention and praise as reinforcing events, the job of guiding their social and intellectual development becomes much easier.

Here are some other examples of ways in which neutral things or events can be made reinforcers:

To teach that money has value, a mother might start by allowing her two-year-old to take a penny, place it in the gum machine, and operate the machine to get the gum. Before long the two-year-old will be asking for "penny . . . penny." The three- or four-year-old might be given a nickel and be allowed to pick out some candies at the grocery store and exchange the nickel for them. Neutral events (coins) followed by reinforcers tend to become reinforcers themselves. Later it is possible for mother to have her child earn points (another learned reinforcer), which are exchanged for money (learned reinforcer), which can be exchanged for treats or a movie.

To teach Pam to handle responsibilities at home, Pam's mother wanted to use gold stars. But to five-year-old Pam, gold stars didn't mean anything. So mother said at breakfast, "Listen, Pam, today when I see you do helpful tasks around the house like tidying up your room, helping me set the table, putting dishes away, or playing nicely with the baby, I'm going to give you a gold star. If you get five gold stars by bedtime, I'll give you a special ice cream bar treat." Gold stars rapidly became interesting and valuable to Pam. Later that week mother put up a chart on the wall with tasks listed as Pam's responsibilities, and mother placed gold stars on the chart for each task completed. Occasionally, mother would get excited about how many stars Pam had earned and decided something special was in order. In this way, gold stars continued to be valuable to Pam, even though they were never directly exchanged for anything.

SOCIAL, TOKEN, AND ACTIVITY REINFORCERS

In learning to use reinforcers effectively, we find it most useful to be clear about three groups of reinforcers that cover most of the cases—social reinforcers, token reinforcers, and activity reinforcers. Social reinforcers are based on *what you do*—tone of voice, physical nearness, attending by looking, saying something nice. Token reinforcers are *things* (points, stars, money, trading stamps) that can be exchanged for a variety of reinforcers (candy, a movie, free time). Activity reinforcers are based on *what your child likes to do*—swing, go for a ride, play ball, play cards, paint, eat. By just concentrating on these three classes of reinforcers, you will find a wealth of ideas on how to readily provide positive consequences for child behavior you want to strengthen.

Social reinforcers keep us all going. You like people who take time to be thoughtful and show appreciation for what you do for them. A "thank you" at the right time may be very conventional, but it can still make a job worthwhile. The majority of parents teaching their children use social reinforcers as rewards. Social reinforcers can be further divided into words of praise, expressions, facial and bodily closeness, and contact. This listing is just a small sample of the possibilities:

WORDS OF PRAISE

"That's a good job."	"Right."
"Wow! You did it!"	"That pleases me."
"Good."	"I wish I could do as well."
"Thanks."	"Let me see you do it
"Terrific!"	again."
"That's paying attention."	"You've really been
"Why don't you show this	working hard."
paper to Father?"	"I'm impressed."

FACIAL AND BODILY EXPRESSIONS

Clap hands	Laugh
Watch carefully	Jump up and down
Smile	Act excited
Nod	Wink

CLOSENESS

Sit together	Go to your child's side
Walk together	Join in his activity
Talk together	Take your child with you some place

CONTACT

Touch	Pick up and hold
Hug	Hold hand
Rock	Shake hand
Scratch back	Stroke or rub arm
Pat on head	

Token reinforcers in the form of money help keep our national and world economies functioning. They also do much to support behavior in school in the form of credits toward graduation. Merchants throughout the United States have found that it helps business if the customers are reinforced with trading stamps that can be exchanged for various products. In the world of children, token reinforcers over the years have taken such forms as a brass ring on the merry-go-round that is good for a free ride, bubble gum cards that can be traded, and bottle caps that can be turned in for a prize. While social reinforcers are behaviors, token reinforcers are objects that can be given and exchanged for other reinforcers. The "good things" tokens are traded for are called backup reinforcers.

POSSIBLE TOKENS

Gold stars	Colored pieces of paper
Checkmarks on a chart	Marbles
Pennies	Beads
Poker chips	Beans

POSSIBLE BACKUP REINFORCERS

Edibles	Play a game with Daddy
Toys	A movie
Special trips	Extra TV time
A story	Horseback riding

While it is valuable to be able to use social and token reinforcers in teaching your child to become an adult, there is still another kind of reinforcer to consider.

Activity Reinforcers can be anything your child likes to do. The beautiful thing about activity reinforcers is that you can learn about them so easily. Just observe your child and see how he spends his time when given a choice. In using activity reinforcers you just need to follow *Grandma's Rule:* FIRST YOU WORK AND THEN YOU PLAY.

You tell your child that after he completes something you want him to do he may do something he wants to do. For example, "You can go out and play when you finish your homework." Some parents get the procedure backwards and say, "You can go out and play if you'll do your homework later." This is a harder contract to keep. It can work if a child has learned to keep his promises. The better procedure, however, is to have the fun behavior follow the work behavior.

The more general principle on which Grandma's Rule is based is this:

Principle 6: Any more-preferred activity can be used to reinforce a less-preferred activity by following the less-preferred activity with the more-preferred activity.

Lloyd Homme (who gave Grandma's Rule its name) demonstrated an unusual use of Grandma's Rule with three young children who liked to run and scream. He wanted to teach them to sit and take instruction in reading. To accomplish this he made a contract: "Sit quietly and watch what I do at the blackboard; then you may run and scream until the timer goes 'bing'." The amount of time for sitting and working was gradually increased. This procedure was very effective in teaching appropriate school behaviors.[3]

It's not too difficult to get Grandma's Rule turned around another way by taking a negative approach. In one family we worked with, mother was battling her son Kenny. Kenny didn't clean up his room as he was supposed to do on Saturday morning, so mother said, "You didn't clean up your room so you can't go out and play." Kenny was angry and pouty all day and still would not clean up his room. He also accused mother of being mean and never hugging him. We suggested that mother try a positive use of Grandma's Rule, rather than punishing Kenny. Tell Kenny that "When you clean up your room, you can go out and play." The very first time she tried it Kenny was a different boy. He got right down to work and finished the job in ten minutes. Mother was now able to compliment him on his good work and give him the hug he wanted. Mother finally knew the difference between a positive and negative approach to discipline.

The use of Grandma's Rule can take many forms, as the following examples illustrate:

"Take your bath and then you can watch TV for 30 minutes."

"You can go to visit Jimmy after you empty the trash."

"Finish eating your carrots and potatoes and you can have desert."

"When everybody is quiet, Father will serve dinner."

"When the dishes are done, we'll go to the movie."

Remember, a key procedure in using any reinforcer is to have the reinforcing event *follow* the behavior you wish to strengthen.

Also remember, when you make a rule about reinforcers be sure to stick to it. If Kenny doesn't make his bed, he doesn't get to go out and play. Consistent application of rules about consequences is essential to making them work.

SETTING CONDITIONS

A final concern in identifying what reinforcers to use in teaching your child has to do with the effects of using a reinforcer on its future reinforcement value. Food is not reinforcing if your stomach is stuffed full. Candy can make you feel sick if you eat too much. In general, too much of a good thing turns it into a bad thing. A reinforcer that is over-used loses its reinforcing power. If Billy has been playing baseball for three hours, the desire for more physical play may not be as great as the desire to rest in front of TV. If you always praise in the same way with the same words, it gets dull and may become ineffective. So the point is that it is necessary to think about what reinforcers are likely to be effective in relation to what has gone on in the past few hours —that is, in terms of the setting conditions under which the reinforcer is to be used.

Principle 7: Repeated use of the same reinforcer in a short time period can decrease its effectiveness.

SUMMING UP

The principle that consequences determine what we do has been with man throughout history. It is the foundation of the free enterprise business system. Yet it is indeed amazing that it has taken 6,000 years to state the principle in such a way that it becomes a useful tool for parents in rearing their children. The goal of this book is to bring to parents an understanding of the power of this principle and other principles of behavior change. In this chapter, we have discussed and illustrated seven principles:

1. To increase the rate of some behavior, follow the behavior with reinforcing consequences.

2. To decrease the rate of some behavior, follow the behavior with a punishing consequence.

3. To decrease the rate of behavior, no longer reinforce it.

4. It is necessary to test any particular consequence to be sure it is a reinforcer or punisher for a particular child.

5. To make a reinforcing stimulus out of a neutral stimulus, repeatedly follow the neutral stimulus with a known reinforcer.

6. Any more-preferred activity can be used to reinforce a less-preferred activity by following the less-preferred activity with the more-preferred activity. (Grandma's Rule).

7. The repeated use of the same reinforcer in a short time period can decrease the effectiveness of that reinforcer.

As a first step in learning to identify, create, and use reinforcers we distinguished between:

Natural reinforcers . . . which come with the baby, and
Learned reinforcers . . . which are created by use of Principle 5.

We also distinguished three classes of reinforcers especially important to parents:

Social reinforcers . . . based on *parent behavior* (praise, touch, nearness, expressions),
Token reinforcers . . . *things* that can be traded for a variety of backup reinforcers, and
Activity reinforcers . . . based on *child behavior*—what he likes to do.

Consequences count. Learn to make them count for you.

3 | *Principles for Using Reinforcers*

Julie was having trouble in school. She was a slow reader and as a sixth grader found it difficult to keep up with her daily assignments. Her grades were near failing and the prospect of being held back worried Julie and her mother. For awhile mother tried working with her each day after school. This just led to Julie relying on mother to do every step for her, so mother gave it up. Next, mother tried using Julie's allowance as a reinforcer. Julie was getting an allowance of fifty cents a week. Mother required that she now earn her allowance through school grades, which came out each six weeks. If all her grades were C or better, she would get three dollars. For each grade above C she could earn a fifty-cents bonus. For Julie, six weeks was a long time to wait for anything. This approach did little to change her daily study habits, except that the week before the six-week grades she seemed to try a little harder. When the six-week grades came out, there was no improvement. Julie got no allowance, mother was furious, and Julie cried for hours. At this point mother sought help through a local clinic.

Reinforcers are not magic. They have to be used with skill and a full knowledge of different kinds of steps to take at different points in learning. In her first attempts to help Julie, mother gave so much assistance that Julie did not have to learn anything. Mother failed to set it up so that she could reward Julie for improvement, a step at a time. In shifting to an allowance based on grades, mother now required Julie to work for six weeks with no rewards (and no allowance, which she had been used to getting). The time between putting out effort in studying and the reinforcer was just too long. The procedure did not work. Julie failed, mother's efforts failed, and no one was happy. Very likely Julie's mother decided that rewards just don't work with a "slow child."

PRINCIPLES FOR USING REINFORCERS

There are three important principles that need to be considered in the use of any reinforcer:

Principle 1: Reinforce immediately in teaching new behavior.

Principle 2: In the early stages of teaching, follow each response with a reinforcer; later in teaching, gradually reinforce fewer and fewer responses in an unpredictable fashion.

Principle 3: Reinforce improvement.

REINFORCE IMMEDIATELY

Behavior is strengthened when it is reinforced. It takes simple logic to infer that if reinforcers are delayed, other behavior may occur and the wrong behavior may be reinforced. In the process, the behavior you want to strengthen may be extinguished. Julie needed to develop some regular study habits for doing her school assignments. Requiring her to wait six weeks for reinforcement was just too long. She did not learn to study and did not improve her grades. Another approach that might work would be to make a chart covering the six-week period. Each subject area for which Julie has regular homework is listed on the chart. Julie's teachers are contacted in setting this up so that mother has a clear picture of the teacher's expectations on homework. For each day in each subject area, Julie can earn up to ten points. The points each day provide for a more immediate reinforcement and her allowance at the end of each week is earned through the points. A regular time each day is agreed on for homework, and points are awarded after mother has checked to see that the work in each area has been done. Praise and special attention are also used to help Julie get going, and help is available where needed. This is the start of a program for Julie that could be more effective.

As a practical matter, it is not always possible for a parent to immediately reinforce every desired response. Fortunately, there are ways to get around this. When children can understand language, it becomes possible to bridge a delay by simply telling your child what he did that you are rewarding him for. And, as illustrated above, token reinforcers (points) and social reinforcers (praise) can be used as the immediate reinforcers with the backup reinforcers delayed until a more appropriate time.

REINFORCE EACH RESPONSE, THEN . . .

The second principle in using reinforcers states that to get behavior going, reinforce each response; to keep behavior going, gradually reinforce fewer and fewer responses in an unpredictable fashion. This principle is based on the fact that new learning occurs most rapidly when each appropriate response is reinforced and on the fact that the persistence of behavior is highest when the schedule of reinforcement is unpredictable. One of the goals of parents should be to teach children to persist in important activities even when the parent is not there to reward them. Persistence can be taught by gradually lessening the giving of reinforcers in an unpredictable way.

For example, to teach Julie to persist in doing her homework, mother might use this procedure. Instead of awarding forty points at the end of the study period, she places a card with forty squares on Julie's study table. Based on teacher requirements, Julie is expected to do about forty minutes of homework each day. Mother tells Julie that if she is working each time mother checks on her, she will earn a point. The points count toward her allowance (or maybe a special treat). Mother then sets a kitchen timer. When the timer rings, she checks Julie. If Julie is working, mother tells her to put a check in one of the squares. In the beginning, the timer is set to ring on the average of once a minute (that is, thirty seconds, one minute, twenty seconds, two minutes, forty-five seconds, etc.). If this works well, the average interval is increased to two minutes (and each check mark is worth two points). Next, mother goes to an average interval of four minutes (and each check mark is worth four points), and then eight minutes. An unpredictable set of times is used and gradually lengthened. Reinforcement occurs less frequently, and Julie slowly learns to work for longer periods on her own. After the eight-minute average time schedule, mother could probably eliminate the timer and tell Julie that she will be checking informally on her studying and give her the points she has earned at the end of the study period.

Young children need to be taught persisting habits in such areas as getting dressed, keeping clean, brushing teeth, and eating the right foods. If the principle for teaching persistent behavior is kept in mind, it means parents should give lots of attention and praise for these behaviors in the beginning and then gradually reduce their attention unpredictably. The same rule will help when it comes to encouraging practice of a violin or piano.

REINFORCE IMPROVEMENT

Julie's mother tried to reinforce improvement by giving three dollars to Julie if she made all C's and bonuses for higher grades. Unfortunately, Julie could not make the first big jump from E's and D's to all C's. As noted earlier, mother also failed to insure that Julie's study behavior was rewarded each day so that she had a chance to improve her grades. An improvement in the procedures used by Julie's mother might be to give so much allowance for each grade in each subject area that is higher than the last time. An improvement from E to D in one area or D to C in another could be rewarded. The key is to set reasonable goals that you know can be achieved and to shoot for higher goals step by step.

Improvement can take many forms. At first, just staying at a study desk for ten minutes may be worthy of reward. Then you might focus on increasing the time spent in studying. Later you might focus on quality of the work done. It is often the case that the first thing we have to praise or otherwise reinforce is *trying*. When a child tries and fails, he should still be praised for trying, because if you can keep him at it he might succeed.

TOKEN REINFORCEMENT SYSTEMS

The use of token systems in the home has many advantages. Their formal nature leads parents and children to spell out agreements with each other in such a way that both parents and children know where they are heading. They permit immediate reinforcement quite readily. They provide an easy method for "thinning" the schedule by requiring more responses for fewer points. They make it possible to use stronger reinforcers when praise does not work without having to constantly feed a child candy or the like. They provide for individual differences among children in determining what is reinforcing by allowing a choice of many backup reinforcers.

As you will see from the examples that follow, most token reinforcement systems have the following components:

1. Tokens that are easy to use.
2. A variety of backup reinforcers.
3. Pricing procedures designed to prevent inflation.
4. An explicit spelling out of how tokens can be earned and spent.
5. Record keeping procedures (graphs of progress, charts of how to earn and spend points).
6. Procedures for getting off the system by shifting to other forms of reinforcement.

TABLE 1. Examples of points Toni could earn each day for completing eight household tasks.

TASK	POINTS
Bed made up—Covers straight, neat and smooth, sheets not visible, pillows covered, blankets folded, no other items on bed.	5
Clothes hung properly—Clothes hung straight on hangers in closet, no hangers on closet door.	5
Personal articles neatly placed—Top of dresser neat, articles arranged in symmetrical array, no powder spilled.	5
Floor swept—No cement dust film on floor. (Home was of cinder block construction in housing project where white powdery dust accumulated quickly.)	5
Straighten and dust living room—Magazines on shelves, TV in place (not where Toni watched it from floor), table cleaned, books in place, no dust on furniture.	10
Kitchen duties—Wash or dry dishes, dishes in cupboard, towel on rack.	20
Bathroom duties—Towel on rack, soap in soap dish, lavatory clean and dry.	20
Odd jobs on request—Clean out car, bring in groceries, sweep off porch.	5–20

TONI LEARNS TO HELP MOTHER

Toni is a ten-year-old girl. For six months, Toni's mother had been trying to get Toni to straighten up her room, sweep the floor, and make her bed. Threats and reminders did no good. Toni's mother enrolled in a course in which the child management principles covered in this book were being taught. She decided to use a point system at home to encourage Toni to learn to carry out her responsibilities.

The first step was to devise a point chart in which each task was carefully specified and points assigned. See the chart on the next page made by Toni's mother.

Note that each task on the list was specified in such a way that Toni and mother could determine if the task was completed right. This helped to eliminate arguments about a half-done job. It also helped Toni understand exactly what mother expected.

It is possible to follow Toni's progress with a graph of the points she earned, kept by Toni's mother. Figure 1 shows how many points Toni earned each day under a number of conditions. Each of these conditions is explained in the discussion that follows.

Baseline₁. At first mother just noted how often Toni completed tasks on the list after telling Toni that mother expected her to help out. In eight days, Toni earned a total of ten points for a 1.25 average per day.

Points. Next, mother placed a graph on the bedroom door and showed Toni the point chart indicating how she could earn points. Each evening they recorded the points together. Over six days, Toni earned an average of 16.7 points, completing two to four tasks a day.

Pennies. Mother now made it possible for Toni to exchange points for pennies. Toni averaged 36.7 points per day.

Baseline₂. As a part of the demonstration (for her class) of the importance of the reinforcers in helping Toni learn

FIGURE 1. The number of points Toni earned each day for performing household tasks. *Baseline₁*—before experimental manipulations. *Points*—graphing the points the subject earned each day. *Pennies*—points were exchanged for pennies at the rate of one penny per point. *Campfire Uniform*—points were exchanged for blouse and skirt of uniform at rate of 400 points per item. *Baseline₂*—reinstatement of Baseline₁. *Christmas Gifts*—points could be exchanged for money toward purchase of Christmas gifts, at rate of one penny per point.

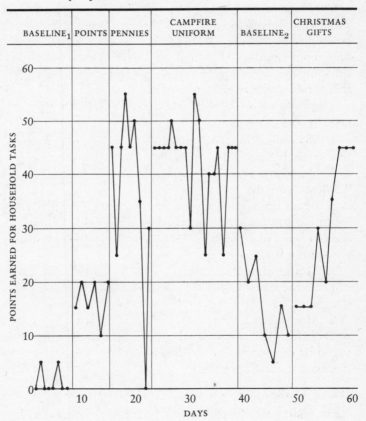

responsibilities, mother decided to stop the system and see if Toni continued with the tasks. Mother told Toni she was running out of graph paper and had to stop until her next paycheck came in. Mother still kept track of the tasks completed by Toni. Toni did less and less each day, averaging 15.6 points a day. This was still three times as much as during the first baseline but declining. One could reasonably expect that without some other procedures to encourage Toni, she would revert to her old nonhelping behavior.

Christmas Gifts. The point system was reinstated and Toni was allowed to earn a penny for each point that could be used to buy Christmas presents. This mean that now and then Toni could go shopping for a gift she wanted to buy for someone else. Toni averaged 29.4 points per day during this period and was still improving.[1]

There are some very important aspects of the procedures used by Toni's mother:

1. She spelled out how points could be earned and what they could be exchanged for.

2. She kept a chart of progress so that she was sure and Toni was sure that a real change was occurring.

3. By using a baseline condition and a "points" only condition (no exchange), mother could tell just which procedures were most helpful. The points alone were not very powerful until backed up with pennies.

4. Mother shifted reinforcers with the seasons and Toni's needs at the time to keep the points earned important to her daughter.

5. Mother set up her point systems so that it was not possible for Toni to earn all the money she could reasonably spend by doing little work. The pricing was fair in terms of the work involved and Toni's desires.

JERRY LEARNS TO WEAR HIS ORTHODONTIC DEVICE

For eight years Jerry's mother had been trying to get him to follow the advice of dentists, but Jerry, now sixteen, still would not wear a two-band device considered essential to correcting his problem. His parents had spent $3,300 in trying to correct his malformation. In desperation, the following experimental program was set up. Initially, mother checked Jerry three to four times daily to see if he was wearing both bands. He was averaging about 25 percent of the time (see Figure 2). Mother then decided to try using praise when she found him wearing the device (she had been criticizing a lot) to see if this would make a difference. While praise for appropriate behavior often is very effective, in this case it was not. So mother next told Jerry that if he was wearing his device when she checked, he could earn twenty-five cents to be paid at the end of the month. He was checked five times a day. If he was not wearing his device, he would lose twenty-five cents. A record was kept on a calendar in the kitchen. Jerry increased wearing his device to 60 percent of the times checked. This was still not good enough, so mother decided to see if *immediate* reinforcement would be better than delayed reinforcement. Under new rules, each time she checked, Jerry would receive twenty-five cents immediately if he was wearing his device and he would lose twenty-five cents if he was not. Under this condition, Jerry wore his device 97 percent of the time. When the monetary reward was withdrawn for five days, Jerry still maintained wearing the device 64 percent of the time. The reward system was reinstated and Jerry returned to nearly 100 percent performance. Mother then "thinned out" the frequency of checks so that only one check a day was being made (and twenty-five cents given). Then only one check was made on the average of every two weeks. After eight months, Jerry's dentist said that great progress had been made so that the device was no longer needed.[2]

Let us review the important procedures used by Jerry's mother:

1. She kept records of progress.
2. She first tried to use an easily available reinforcer—

FIGURE 2. A record of the percentage of time Jerry used an orthodontic device. Measurements were taken five times a day at varying intervals. *Baseline₁*—before experimental manipulations. *Social Reinforcement*—ignoring subject when he was not wearing the device and praising him when he was. *Delayed Monetary Payoff*—paying youngster 25 cents when he had apparatus in place during an observation and charging him 25 cents when it was not in place. Monetary exchange took place at end of month. *Immediate Monetary Payoff₁*—same as Delayed Monetary Payoff except that money was exchanged immediately after each check. *Baseline₂*—reinstatement of Baseline₁. *Immediate Monetary Payoff₂*—reinstatement of Immediate Monetary Payoff₁. *Post Checks*—periodic checks after termination of formal experiment.

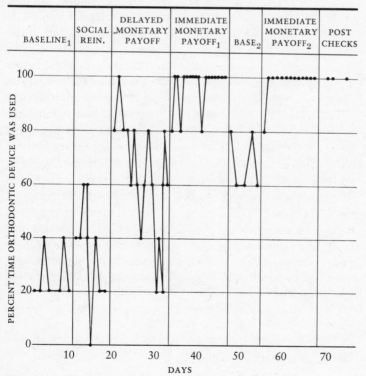

praise—before deciding that a stronger reinforcer was needed.

3. Since she had records of progress, she could determine that her first reward procedure—delayed reward—was not working well enough. She was in a position to try again.

4. Immediate reinforcement worked better.

5. Once consistent performance had been established with immediate reinforcement, she gradually thinned out the frequency of reinforcement to once a day and then even to once every two weeks. Checking now and then and giving a quarter helped maintain the behavior once it had been well established.

6. For an older boy, a fairly large monetary reward (twenty-five cents for each check) was chosen, although mother might have also been successful with a ten-cent reward.

A Point System for the Walker Family

In our clinical work with families, we have often been impressed with how overwhelming the task of rearing three or four children can be when both parents work or both are involved in lots of activities. The next example illustrates a point system applied to three children in the Walker family to help bring some order into their lives. George was nine, Dollie was eight, and Keith was five. Mr. Walker was a college graduate, and Mrs. Walker was a college student majoring in nursing.

George was a good student but had taken to skipping school and was a problem at home and school. He was sassy toward mother and often failed to follow directions.

Dollie had mild cerebral palsy and attended a class for educable retarded children at school. She had been given a great deal of speech therapy. She was said to be hyperactive, and occasionally she threw tantrums.

Keith's only problem according to his parents was that he whined too much.

The children bickered much of the time, and the boys engaged in a lot of horseplay at bedtime.

In an interview with a psychologist, the parents discussed the responsibilities they expected for each of their children and the kinds of privileges the children might like. A tentative list was drawn up and points assigned, as shown in Table 2.

The children could earn basic privileges daily, such as use of TV, bicycle, playing outside, bedtime story, and games with parents. Extra points could be saved for a movie, a picnic, or treats. As needed, other kinds of privileges or tickets could be added to the list.

Behaviors that could occur each day, such as making beds, could earn points when completed or lose points if not completed. Some tasks that could not occur with regularity could only earn points (for example, sweeping the rug). Some behaviors that were particularly disturbing to the parents were fined (bickering, for instance). Since fines are a form of punishment, we will not discuss their effects in any detail in this chapter, but will in Chapter Five.

Records were kept on the performance of tasks for about one month before the point system was introduced. George occasionally cleaned his room, but otherwise most helping tasks were not performed by any of the children. With the introduction of the point system, helping tasks were consistently performed each day. Fines were also found to be effective in reducing the bickering, teasing, jumping on furniture, whining, and bedtime horseplay.[4]

The important new procedures illustrated in this study were:

1. The idea of basic privileges being earned each day.

2. The notion that with slight modification, a group of children could be on the same basic system.

3. The notion that fines might be appropriate for some behaviors.

TABLE 2. Walker Family Point System[3]
(Partial list)

TICKETS AVAILABLE	PRICE IN POINTS
Basic privileges	60
Drive-in-movie	200
Picnic	50
Ice cream bar	25
Candy bar	25
Make cookies	35

BEHAVIORS THAT EARNED OR LOST POINTS	POINTS EARNED OR LOST
George: Make bed	10
Hang up clothes	10
Clean room	20
Feed dog	20
Keith: Empty trash	20
Set silver and napkins for dinner	20
Brush teeth	20
Dollie: Make bed	20
Feed cat	20
Bathe	20

BEHAVIORS THAT EARNED POINTS	POINTS EARNED
Sweep rug	10
Clean bathroom	20
Answer telephone	15

BEHAVIORS THAT LOST POINTS	POINTS LOST
Bickering	10
Teasing	10
Whining	10

APPLICATION OF TOKENS IN SCHOOLS

Our final two illustrations are intended to acquaint parents with the potential importance of using token reinforcement systems in working with the hard-to-teach child or potential dropouts in the school. In the past few years a large number of very ingenious token reinforcement programs have been tested to show that school can be made important to children who have not succeeded with more traditional methods.

A PROGRAM FOR DROPOUTS

Montrose Wolf and his colleagues at the University of Kansas[5] set up a program for sixteen pupils from a low-income area of Kansas City, Kansas. After school each day, the children came to a three-hour remedial program. They also came in the summer. Another group of children with the same problems and skills was left in the regular school system to serve as a comparison group.

The token system they devised worked like this. The students were given cards marked off into squares. Whenever points were earned, the instructor would place a mark in a square. Filled cards could be traded for a variety of goods and activities such as snacks, candy, trips, novelties, or even long-range goals like a second-hand bicycle.

At first, points could be earned for every problem solved in arithmetic or every question answered in reading. As skill developed, the children were required to do more work for fewer points. The instructor bargained with each child on the points that he could earn, the object being to help each child derive success while encouraging maximum performance.

Some other rewards were also used. For example, if grades at school increased, those showing improvement had a special party. Attendance and good school behavior as reported by regular school teachers could also earn bonus points.

These children had shown median gains on achievement tests of .6 grade levels in the previous two years. With the token program in effect, the children gained 1.5 grade levels. The comparison group gained .8 grade levels. Changes in attitudes, work habits, and grades were also noted by their regular teachers.

A School Program for Maladjusted Children

O'Leary and Becker[6] established a token program in a public school classroom containing seventeen problem children from economically deprived homes. The children showed severe behavior problems and were several years behind in basic skills. Averaging nine years in age, most of them were just beginning to learn to read.

At the beginning of the study, observations taken on eight of the seventeen children revealed that they were off-task (showing disruptive behaviors) an average of 76 percent of the time. Figure 3 shows the daily percentage of off-task behavior before the token system was started (days one through ten). The teacher in this class was young, dedicated, and usually exhausted at the end of each day. She was unable to accomplish much in the way of teaching, because the children paid little attention to her.

A special token program was begun for the period from 12:30 to 2:00 each day on day eleven. A few simple rules were placed on the board such as, "In seat," "Pay attention," "Work hard," "Raise hand to talk." Small ten-cent notebooks were taped on each desk to record points in. The teacher explained that every fifteen minutes, she would stop the lesson and award from zero to ten points to each child. The more carefully the children followed the rules and showed improvement, the more points they could earn. Points could be exchanged for candy, kites, small toys, marbles, crayons, and so forth. With more points, a child could choose from a better selection of prizes. At first, prizes

FIGURE 3. Average percentage of deviant behavior during base and token periods for eight children.

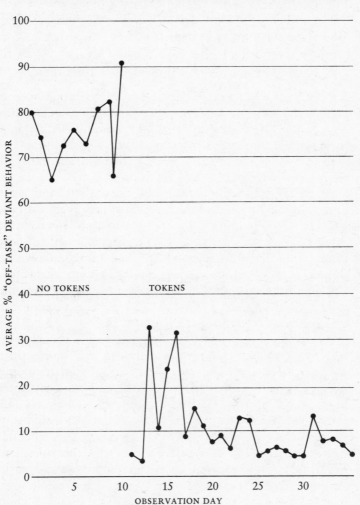

were earnable each day. Then the children had to learn to save points for two, three, and four days; and the number of points needed for a given prize was increased.

As can be seen in Figure 3, when the token system was introduced the children's behavior improved dramatically. Off-task behavior dropped to less than 10 percent. Since praise was given with points, the children also began to respond to praise from the teacher. Seeing their own progress, they also began to take pride in learning. The children were reported to be well behaved in other school settings and attendance improved. The cost of the prizes was $86.76 over eight weeks. This was a lot cheaper than providing psychotherapy and most likely more effective.

A CAUTION

Just because strong reinforcers work well, that does not mean that you should use them all of the time. In fact, you should not use any stronger reinforcers than are needed to get the job done. Use praise and attention when they are enough to make things work. Only go to strong reinforcers when weak reinforcers fail. The reason for this is that we usually want children to be motivated by social reinforcers in interactions with teachers and other adults. We need to use procedures that will insure that children are responsive to a variety of social reinforcers. Even when strong reinforcers are used for awhile, they should be paired with praise and attention and then gradually reduced as the social reinforcers become more effective.

SUMMING UP

Three key principles in the effective use of reinforcers are:
1. Reinforce immediately in teaching new behaviors.

2. In the early stages of teaching, follow each response with a reinforcer; later in teaching, gradually reinforce fewer and fewer responses.

3. Reinforce improvement.

The use of these principles has been illustrated with a variety of examples, including token reinforcer systems. Token systems provide a vehicle for giving reinforcers immediately and for shifting the frequency of use of reinforcers relatively easily. By providing for a choice of backup reinforcers, token systems also allow for individual differences in what is reinforcing.

A good token system has these components:

1. Tokens that are easy to use.

2. A variety of backup reinforcers.

3. Pricing procedures designed to prevent inflation (where the child has so many tokens to spend that they lose their value).

4. Record keeping procedures (graphs of progress, charts of how to earn and spend points).

5. Procedures for getting off the system by shifting to other forms of reinforcement.

Although not explicitly mentioned, the use of a token system has another advantage for parents. The agreements with your child to give points under various conditions will set it up so that you are reminded of your goals and cued to keep working on them. Often, without such aids, good intentions go for naught.

4 | *On Becoming a Reinforcing Parent*

In Chapters Two and Three we outlined and illustrated some basic principles in taking a positive approach to children. But reading about principles and believing they are important is not enough if you don't know what to do in specific situations. This chapter illustrates some of the pitfalls and solutions for parents who want to become more positive with their children. The first step is to gain an understanding of what goes wrong with a negative approach. The next step is to begin to specify how you should behave differently, and then set up a program to teach yourself to become more positive.

PROBLEMS WITH NEGATIVE APPROACH

The most common negative approach to children consists of verbal criticism and threats. In our experimental studies of the effects of teacher behavior on problem behavior in the classroom, the way in which teachers use praise and criticism has been found to be an extremely important factor in how the children behave. Consider the following case study.

Mrs. Johnson was a young first-grade teacher who had been teaching for three years. Observations in her classroom revealed that she had very poor control over her children. For example, when she was working with her reading group, many of the other children would not stay in their seats; some were whistling and some were hitting and pushing. Loud talking often interfered with the reading group's lesson. When the children got in line for recess, there was a lot of pushing and hitting. Mrs. Johnson would seem to put up with this increasing chaos for awhile until it got out of hand, and then she would "blow the whistle." "I'm going to turn out the lights and count to ten, and if everyone is not quiet and in their seats, no recess." Sometimes she would just threaten to count to ten. Sometimes she would just stand up, go to the middle of the room, and glare at the children until they quieted down. The children would become a little sullen and quiet for a few minutes, and Mrs. Johnson would return to her reading group. But slowly over the next ten minutes the noise and movement would increase to the point where it was intolerable again.

Two boys in this room averaged 70 percent off-task behavior over five weeks of observation. Mrs. Johnson was observed to almost always use criticism for misbehavior and seldom praised good behavior. After five weeks of observation, Mrs. Johnson was helped to learn some new procedures that involved taking a *positive approach*. She was to follow these three procedures:

1. She was to tell the children what she expected of them by stating a few positive classroom rules. The rules were to be repeated as often as needed as reminders.

2. She was to ignore misbehavior unless someone was getting hurt.

3. She was to focus on good behavior shown by the children and use lots of praise to reinforce it.

To our surprise, during the first week in which these new procedures were tried, Mrs. Johnson had a very difficult time. She didn't know what to do or say when it came to being positive with children. We had to teach her how to do this by taking examples of situations that had happened in her room and having her practice two or three different ways she might have responded to each example. It took several weeks before she felt comfortable being a reinforcing person. As she became more positive in her approach, she was amazed at the change in her classroom. Five or six very active boys became good classroom workers. The two hyperactive boys being observed decreased their off-task behavior from 70 percent to 22 percent. Mrs. Johnson even became aware of several shy children in the classroom who needed, and could now receive, special encouragement from her. There seemed to be an important lesson here: *The more the teacher attended to and criticized the misbehavior, the more misbehavior she got; the more she attended to and praised appropriate behavior, the more appropriate behavior she got.*[1]

Becker and his colleagues, then at the University of Illinois, pursued this problem experimentally to see what was going on. In a study with Madsen,[2] they examined how often children stood up when the teachers had told them to sit down. They found that the more frequently the teachers told the children to sit down, the more frequently the children stood up. This occurred even though the children sat down when told to. The teacher's attention to the standing, by asking the children to sit down, served to reinforce standing.

In another study with Thomas,[3] a teacher was asked to control her use of praise and criticism through several experimental conditions. The class was initially very well behaved, and the teacher used a lot of praise to keep her students working. When all praise was stopped and a low level of criticism maintained, the children increased their off-task behavior from 9 percent to 25 percent. When criticism was increased from five times every twenty minutes to sixteen times every twenty minutes, off-task behavior went as high as 50 percent and averaged 31 percent. Criticism for off-task behavior functioned as a reinforcer and increased off-task behavior. A return to the use of much praise brought the class back to a high level of on-task behavior.

In Chapter Two, it was noted that Danny's mother got a lot of commanding behavior out of Danny when she responded to commands, and she got a lot of cooperative behavior when she responded to cooperative responses. Similarly, Rorey's mother gave excessive attention to Rorey's misbehavior and that is what she got until a change was made in her behavior with Rorey. The same effect of attention to negative behavior found in the classroom with teachers is found at home with parents. The parent who primarily attempts to train a child with scolding and criticism is likely to find he or she has a lot of problem behavior to deal with. This is not to say that there is not a time and place for scolding and criticism in training children, it just means that an exclusive focus on misbehavior is unlikely to be effective. Becker and colleagues[4] have called this phenomena the CRITICISM TRAP. The basic sequence is this:

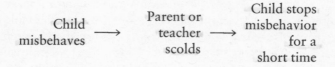

Child misbehaves → Parent or teacher scolds → Child stops misbehavior for a short time

Scolding follows misbehavior and cues the child to stop for the present or something worse might happen. But the scolding has actually provided attention to the misbehavior (reinforcing it) and the misbehavior occurs more frequently in the future. This is a trap, because the parent thinks the scolding works when the child stops temporarily. That is, the parent is reinforced for scolding by the child's stopping temporarily. But the parent has reinforced the behavior she is trying to stop, and the long-range effect (in contrast to the immediate effect) is an increase in the misbehavior.

The criticism trap arises because parents or teachers focus on misbehavior and not on the positive teaching of behavior needed to become an adult. If from the start, parents would set out objectives for what they would like their children to be able to do at a given age and teach toward those goals, they would not have the misbehavior to focus on.

TAKING A POSITIVE APPROACH

A positive approach involves having positive goals for your child and reinforcing progress toward those goals. Changing your own behavior to make it more positive is not an easy task, but it can be done. It is necessary to understand what is involved and how to engineer your environment so that it will support your new learning.

The steps to take are these:

1. *Understand the importance of focusing on positive goals.* The past few pages should have provided this.

2. *Learn to set positive objectives for children at various ages.* This is a more difficult task, but later in this book we attempt to show how to do this in a variety of areas of concern to parents.

3. *Learn to use reinforcers frequently and skillfully.* Chapters Two and Three have provided a start in this direction. Some further guidelines and practice are provided in the rest of this chapter. Three substeps are involved:

Set up the environment to provide cues and reminders.

Set up the environment to reinforce your change to using a more positive approach.

Practice different ways to use praise and other reinforcers skillfully.

Reinforcers: Cues and Reminders

A common problem for busy parents is that they get so involved with some task that they forget they are trying to be more positive until it is too late. Well, anticipate the problem and arrange things so that you can't forget. Put up signs in the bathroom and on the refrigerator to remind yourself to praise more.

Another good procedure is to use a token system even though you don't really need it. Prepare a chart explaining how tokens can be earned and spent and make a graph of daily progress. Then use tokens that you can physically give to your child, such as poker chips or pennies. The rule is this: praise your child *before* giving the token. What did he do that you liked? Tell him about it and then give him the poker chip. If you set it up right, your child will start *reminding you* that he has been doing a good job that you didn't notice. The charts and graph on the wall and the tokens in your pocket will also remind you to find behaviors to praise. Use of a token system provides you with cues to help get the process going.

One parent with four aggressive boys tried for three months to learn to praise cooperative behavior, but she just could not get it going. She still found herself jumping on the boys with threats and punishments *after* they had been in a fight. Finally, it was suggested that she try a token system. The tokens were squares of colored paper—a different color for each boy. The boys were told that if they earned five tokens a day for a week they would get special treats, such as a trip to an amusement park. Mother had to watch the boys a lot more carefully to find twenty times during the day to praise them and give out tokens. If she got lax, the boys would let her know it. Before long, she got used to focusing on the positive and did not need the tokens any more.

Reinforcing the Reinforcer

Since your behavior is also a function of consequences, it

is important to find ways to get reinforcement for a change in your behavior. Here are three ways for this to happen:

1. Measure a change in your child's behavior.
2. Measure a change in your own behavior.
3. Have another family member take notes of your behavior and let you know when it is better.

Suppose you set up a token system as suggested in the last chapter. Your goal is to learn to praise more and focus on positive objectives. Your point system helps you specify those positive objectives and you follow the rule to remark on praiseworthy behavior when giving out tokens. Now you simply need to record the number of objectives your child completes each day. If you do this before you start the new system (a baseline period), as well as during the new system, you will be able to see for yourself that it is working. This kind of evidence is reinforcing to most parents. The effect will be to reinforce a more positive approach.

Another approach is to get a counter, such as those used to add up purchases in the supermarket or a golf-score counter, and use it to record how often you praise your child from the time he comes home from school until bedtime each day. Without trying to be more positive, just find out about your current behavior. Then set about increasing your positive behavior, clicking your counter each time you praise. The evidence of progress can be reinforcing. If the evidence shows no progress, that too can be useful in cueing you to try harder or to try another approach. One teacher we know had a very hard time learning to be more positive in the classroom. We finally made progress with her by giving her a golf-score counter to wear and asking her to record how often she used praise during every fifteen-minute period. She would click the counter each time she used praise and reset it each fifteen minutes after recording the count. In this way, she knew what kind of progress she was making toward a goal of one praise comment a minute.

The third approach goes something like this. Discuss your goal with your husband or wife, being very specific about what would constitute a change. For example, "I praise Jimmy for improved eating habits at least twice during the evening meal," or "I comment on the boys' cooperative behavior at least three times between dinner and bedtime." Then set up some kind of a contract or agreement with your spouse such as, "If I reach my goal for five days in a row during the next seven days, you agree to take me out to dinner. If I fail to reach my goal, I will scratch your back for twenty minutes on each day that I fail." Set up a reward and "punishment" condition in the contract. Furthermore, and most important, have an accounting of progress each evening before going to bed or at some other suitable time.

Understanding that your own behavior is a function of consequences puts you in a position to engineer a situation in which you can get reinforcement for changes in your own behavior. Although it may not seem so at first glance, this is a form of self-control.

Using Praise Skillfully

If you are afraid of children or don't know how to play with them, it is not likely that you will learn to interact more skillfully with them through a book. You might want to get some help through a child guidance clinic. On the other hand, if you are like most parents, you probably just need to know more specifically about what to do, and practice it, to become more effective in using reinforcers.

When reinforcers are used skillfully, they are hardly even noticed. They seem to be a natural part of the interaction between parent and child. Though seeming natural, they are learned skills. They have been learned from watching our own parents or through extensive experience with children. Basic to the skillful use of reinforcers is the communication of a positive attitude through a smile, flirting eyes, a touch, or playfulness. These are the kinds of behaviors that let your children know you care for them and like them. A good reinforcer is a loving parent, expressing this love to show pleasure with a child's progress.

In general, just taking a positive approach to training goals will facilitate your progress in becoming a good reinforcer. When you focus on goals to be rewarded when reached, rather than problem behaviors to be punished, your child will be more inclined to pay attention to what you say and try to please you. The result is you will have more opportunities to practice letting your child know he is doing a good job.

More specific strategies and procedures for making your positive approach effective are these:

1. **Get excited.** Don't be afraid to get a little excited to show you are pleased. Ham it up a little, move your arms, put inflections in your speech, give a hug.

- Kathy, eight, came home with a passing grade in math after three consecutive failing grades. She had been working hard on improvement. When her father came home, her mother told him about it with Kathy present.

  "Wow, Kathy, you really did it! Unbelievable." (He threw his arms out in expression.) "I am so delighted that your hard work paid off. I know how hard you have been working." (He reached down and put his hands under Kathy's arms and tossed her in the air, catching her in a hug.) "I want to see that report card right now."

2. **Use variety in praising.** When you mechanically say the same old thing, it doesn't mean as much and doesn't convey excitement. To learn to use variety, first review the kinds of praise and gestures possible, as outlined in Chapter Two. Then choose two or three situations a day in which you are going to try to use praise with your child, and practice some things you might say ahead of time so that you are ready to

try something new. (Note that point three below also helps in learning to use variety in praising.)

- Tommy is learning to tell you when he needs to go "pee pee." You want to be sure to praise him each time he does tell you. So you decide to practice some ways in which you can praise Tommy.
  —"What a big boy to tell Mommy," and give a hug.
  —"You remembered to tell Mommy. Thanks."
  —"Thanks for telling Mommy. Let's hurry and go and maybe we can find a candy treat."
  —"Great! You told Mommy 'Pee pee.' Good boy."
  —"Tommy remembered! I sure appreciate that."
- Tommy is eating with his spoon and doesn't spill.
  —"Father, did you see Tommy use his spoon just now? He didn't spill a drop."
  —"Gee, Tommy, you are using your spoon just like Mommy and Daddy and not spilling."
  —"Good, Tommy, you got it all in your mouth. Let me see you do it again."
  —"Good, Tommy. You certainly are learning to be careful with your spoon."
  —(Looking under the table and then up at Father.) "I can't believe it. There's no food on the floor. Where did it all go, Tommy?" Tommy pats his stomach. They laugh.

3. **Praise behavior, not the person.** An important key to effective praise is to make it *behavior specific*. When you tell your child exactly what you are praising him for, he will have no doubt about your goal and what he is working on. But there is another benefit. As Haim Ginott points out in *Between Parent and Child*,[5] too often we praise the whole person in generalities that could not possibly be true, such as:

"Such a darling child."
"You're really a smart boy."
"What an angel."
"You certainly are intelligent."

Just consider the situation in which someone has told you how fantastic you are and you didn't believe it. You know differently. Sometimes you do things the right way and sometimes you goof. You're human like anybody else. When praise is made behavior specific, it comes out being believable and is more likely to work as a reinforcer.

- *The wrong way.* Mary brings home a test paper in social studies with a B grade on it. This is the first B she has had all year. Mother says, "What a smart girl to get a B." Mary starts to cry, "I'm *not* smart." Her experience all year has taught her that she does not do as well as other kids. This one exception is not enough to convince her she is smart. It is a lie.
- *The right way.* Mary brings home a test paper in social studies with a B grade on it. Mother looks it over carefully, reading each answer. "Mary, you got plusses on eight of the ten questions. That's really good! And look, your teacher commented on three of them that your answers were thoughtful and complete." Mary cannot deny that what her mother said is true, because the evidence is right there. She is pleased with herself and accepts the praise with a smile.

The key to making praise specific to the behavior is to observe carefully what your child is doing or has done and to describe what you have seen that pleases you. Your child will know you have been paying attention to him by the descriptive observations you make.

Here are a few more examples of descriptive praise:

- "Thanks for cleaning up your room. You made your bed neatly, put your shoes in order, hung up your clothes, and straightened out your books. That's a big help to me."
- "That's what I call good eating. You ate all of your meat, your potatoes, and peas. Would you like some ice cream?"
- "I watched you working on your homework. You really

stayed with it for thirty minutes. How many arithmetic problems did you get done?"

"All twenty of them."

"That's fast."

- "That's a good baseball swing. You held the bat back off your shoulder, watched the ball carefully, and met it with a level swing."

4. **Use activities of the day as reinforcers.** The day in the life of a child is full of possibilities when it comes to activity reinforcers. There are eating times, play times, trips, family games, helping mother, watching TV, making cookies, music, art activities, and so forth. If you keep in mind your teaching goals for your child, you can often use these activities as reinforcers for the skills you want your child to learn. You just have to think ahead a little and set it up so that the events are in fact consequences for good performances.

- "Mommy is going to the store. Hurry and get yourself dressed and you can go with me."
- "There's a Walt Disney special on TV tonight. If you get working on your homework now, you will be able to see it."
- "As soon as you take out the trash, you can help me make cookies."
- "I'll play catch with you as soon as your chores are done."
- "If everyone helps me finish cleaning up the house, we will be able to start for the picnic sooner."
- "As soon as Jimmy finishes his meat, I'll cut the cake."
- "When the table is cleared and clean and the dishwasher loaded, we can play cards."
- "After you get your pajamas on, wash your face, and brush your teeth, I'll read you a story."
- "When you finish your homework, you can go out and play."

Remember to use Grandma's Rule, but don't do it in a bargaining way. Set up opportunities for your child, as illus-

trated. For the last example above, you could have said,
"You can't go out and play until you finish your homework." This makes you the boss imposing on your child,
and he or she might just learn to fight that with some coun-
ter-bargaining. Opportunities invite your child to work for
them. The child has an option of not doing the task if he
doesn't want the reinforcer. But the key is the attitude con-
veyed by focusing on opportunities. "This is really a good
thing. You'd be foolish to pass it up."

5. **When you must correct, try to praise first.** When we
open a communication with criticism, we run a good risk of
not communicating much at all. Focusing on the negative can
lead your child to tune you out so that he misses what you
are trying to teach. So start off by commenting on the things
your child is doing right whenever this is possible.

- David comes to breakfast dressed for school except that
  he hasn't combed his hair. Mother says, "Glad to see
  you're ready so early, David. That shirt looks good on
  you."
  "Thanks," said David.
  "By the way, did you know you forgot to comb your
  hair?"
  "Oops. Be right back."

Contrast the above with this scene:

- David comes in as above. Mother says, "David, your
  hair is not combed. You can't go to school looking like
  that."
  David pouts. "That's not important. I'll get it later."
  "You go do it right now," mother insists.
  Everyone is ready for morning indigestion.

- Gary used his father's tools (with permission) to make a
  skate scooter. However, he left the tools all over the
  garage floor when he was through. Father comes in
  while Gary is riding his new scooter. Father parks in
  the driveway and gets out.
  "Let me see that thing." Father examines the scooter

carefully. "You did a careful job, Gary. The way you braced the handle and upright part will make it last."

"Thanks, Dad."

"Now if you'll put my tools away, I'll be able to put the car in the garage."

"Sure, Dad. Sorry I forgot."

It is not hard to imagine a more typical scene that starts out with a scolding for leaving the tools all over and ends with bad feelings on both sides.

6. **When your child is involved in play, provide a buffer.** Kids, like adults, don't like to be interrupted. Intrusions are irritating and can intensify a negative reaction. The thoughtful parent recognizes this and provides a warning and a little buffer time when an activity must be ended. It also helps to make the upcoming activity as desirable as possible.

- Timmy has set up his blocks, cars, and play village in the family room as bedtime approaches. He is playing intently, driving his cars and trucks through the streets (block roads) of the village. Father gets down on the floor with Timmy and enters his play.

  "I'm going to take my pickup into the garage for servicing," Father says.

  "I have to stop at the store for some bread," says Timmy.

  "All fixed, time to drive home." Father pretends to drive his pickup home. "Bedtime is coming, Timmy. In about five minutes I want you to start putting your toys away and then get ready for bed. Mother's got a treat for you when your things are picked up and you're in your pajamas."

  Timmy asked what the treat was, but Father said it was a surprise. He would have to wait to find out. Timmy started cleaning up right then.

7. **Give a choice.** You can take the sting out of some activities that a child may not especially want to do by clearly giving a choice between two alternatives acceptable to you.

This often makes it unnecessary to force an issue.

- Mary Ann wants to watch TV, but it's bedtime. Mother gives her this choice. "Look, honey, I want you to go and get ready for bed now. After you're ready, you can decide whether you want your story or want to finish watching this show, but you have to be in bed by 8:30."

  Mary Ann hurried to get ready and decided to see the TV show tonight instead of hearing her usual bedtime story.

8. **Use surprises.** Keep a bag of tricks up your sleeve that you use when you need a little extra help to keep things positive. Surprises can make a game out of many distasteful activities. Surprises might include a special toy, something different in a treat, a new game, a fun thing to do . . . almost anything that is a tangible or activity reinforcer. The key is to be suggestive of something special coming, but don't tell what it is until the right time.

SUMMING UP

When parents or teachers focus on undesired behaviors, that's what they get. When the focus is positively placed on desired behaviors, that's what happens. Learning to be more positive requires that you learn to set positive objectives for your child. The objectives are skills or behaviors you want your child to learn. It also requires that you learn how to use various reinforcers skillfully. This latter goal can be facilitated if you:

1. Set up your environment to provide cues and reminders to be more positive. Put up signs, charts, and graphs.

2. Set up your environment to reinforce your change to a more positive approach. Measure a change in your behavior or your child's behavior or get your spouse to keep track of changes in your behavior.

3. Practice different ways of using reinforcers more skill-fully. Besides using more smiles, eye contact, touch, and general playfulness, it was suggested that some of the following be worked on:

- Getting excited when your child pleases you.
- Using variety in praising.
- Praising specific behavior, not the person.
- Using activities of the day as reinforcers.
- When correcting, trying to praise some other behavior first.
- Providing a buffer time for ending an activity when your child is involved in play.
- Giving a choice you can live with when dealing with an activity a child might not really want to do.
- Using surprises.

Remember, don't stop with just reading this chapter. Plan to practice using these ideas in your daily interactions. Write down two things you want to try tomorrow. Then tomorrow night prepare to try two more. Unless you practice new behaviors, you don't learn them.

5 | *Principles for Using Punishment*

The area of punishment probably has more misunderstanding and strong feeling connected with it than any other in behavior theory. Some believe that it is immoral to use punishment. Many believe that punishment does not work because it only reduces the problem behavior temporarily. In the mind of a parent of a two-year-old, however, there can be no doubt that the use of punishment is the moral thing to do when the safety of a two-year-old is at stake. As to punishment working, the facts show that it does work when used intelligently.

PUNISHING EVENTS

In Chapter Two, we presented the basic principle of punishment: to decrease the rate of some behavior, follow the behavior with a punishing event. Many investigations of behavior have shown a good consistency in the kinds of events that serve as punishers. For most human beings, such things as loud noises (yelling) and pain-producing stimulation (a spanking) naturally function as punishers. Also, the taking away of reinforcers (loss of privileges or fines) can, when used appropriately, be punishing events. Finally, events that just precede the occurrence of punishment can become learned punishers. These latter events we usually think of as "Don't signals," such as "No," "Don't," and "Stop." Although there is a good consistency in what will function as punishers for most children, it is necessary to *test out* any particular punisher to find out if it works for a given child.

To get some feel for the effectiveness of punishment, look at some of your moment-by-moment interactions with the physical environment. You learn to walk in ways that avoid the punishment of falling or bumping. You learn not to touch fire. You try not to get into a cold shower. You stop eating after awhile to avoid the discomfort of being too full. Most of the naturally punishing consequences of behavior are learned readily because the consequences are immediate and consistent. It is primarily in the area of socially-administered punishment (people punishing people) that problems are encountered.

PROBLEMS IN USE OF PUNISHMENT

When punishment involving painful events is applied by parents to children, more can occur than the simple weakening of the punished behavior. First, a punished child (like a puppy) will learn to avoid sources of punishment and will try to escape if avoidance fails. This phenomenon has been described as "leaving the field." When the child "leaves the field," the parent loses some control over the future development of the child. Punishing adults can teach children such avoidance and escape behaviors as lying, cheating, concealing, and running away.

Punishment can also generate fear of the parent and anger toward the parent. These feelings are hardly desirable outcomes of childrearing. Finally, pain-inducing punishment, such as spankings, give the child a model of how to use physical aggression to control the behavior of others. Since children often learn to imitate their parents, this could be a source of instruction in aggression.

Because of these problems, the use of direct physical punishment should be avoided under most circumstances. One exception is in teaching young children basic rules of safety. The young child cannot readily avoid or escape from the parent, and the parent can have enough positive contact to undo any negative affects generated by use of punishment. With the young child, make your use of punishment very specific in teaching avoidance of dangers. Punish immediately, use a "Don't signal," be calm, and *aim* the punishment at the response to be avoided. For example, if a child is actually reaching to open drawers with knives in them, try to catch him in the act of reaching. Say, "No. Knives" and slap the reaching hand. Then explain, "Knives can hurt you." If your child is going into the street when he shouldn't, catch him moving toward the street and stop him with a loud "No. Street." Then turn him around and give a couple of spanks to move him back to the play yard. Explain that "Cars can hurt you."

Another exception to the avoidance of physical punishment is in teaching about fire and hot things. In this case you can control the hurt so that a little natural hurt is experienced and provides the punishment. This procedure accomplishes two things. It can teach the meaning of "X can hurt you," and it can teach avoidance of the specific danger. For example, if your baby starts to open a hot oven door, you can say, "No. Hot." Then immediately take his hand and briefly touch it to the door so that he can feel the heat but not get burned. "See, it can hurt you." A similar procedure is effective with boiling water and stove burners.

GENERAL PRINCIPLES

The basic problem in most situations in which one might want to use punishment is that the behavior of the person to be punished has been or is being reinforced. For example, Johnny comes home from school late because he is reinforced by playing games with his friends on the way. Once this is realized, it should be clear that punishment would have to be used forever to counter the potential reinforcement if only punishment were used. It is just this kind of situation that led many people in the past to say that punishment is not effective. Because the punished behavior was being reinforced, stopping the punishment led to a return of the behavior. Fortunately, there are two strategies for not allowing this to happen.

Principle 1: Give reinforcement for behavior incompatible with the punished response.

Principle 2: Be sure the undesired behavior is no longer reinforced.

If mother focuses attention, praise, and other reinforcers on playing in the backyard play area and is vigilant to punish any leaving, the leaving will decrease and the staying will increase. Staying in the play area is incompatible with running into the street. A child cannot do both of them at the same time. Therefore, the more he stays in the yard, the less he can run in the street.

A third principle in the effective use of punishment follows from the undesired side effects of presenting painful events as punishment and from the fact that the stopping of a punishing state can be used as a reinforcer:

Principle 3: Generally punish by withdrawing reinforcers (rather than presenting painful events), but be sure to specify a way to earn them back.

This principle is brought home dramatically in the case study of Claire as presented by Thorne, Tharp, and Wetzel.[1]

Claire was a 16-year-old girl who was referred to a clinic for truancy, poor grades, and "incorrigibility" at home. Claire was about to be expelled from high school. Her mother had tried to bring Claire around by taking away all money, use of the telephone, and dating privileges. She had, however, provided no way for Claire to earn them back. The treatment procedure (the potential effectiveness of which mother questioned) provided that Claire could earn telephone privileges each day by bringing home a note showing that she had attended all classes. If she earned four notes in a week, she could have one weekend date. Five notes earned two nights out. Claire attended school regularly from the first day of the new plan. Before long, notes were sent on Wednesday and Friday only (each good for one weekend night out), and the telephone was made available. After seven more weeks, the notes were stopped and Claire continued to attend school to earn privileges without notes.

A fourth principle is aimed at establishing learned punishers:

Principle 4: Use a "Don't signal" as a warning one time. If the warning is not heeded, back it up with an effective punisher.

"Don't signals" give the parent of a young child a relatively mild way of telling about new dangers to be avoided. "Don't signals" are learned punishers. They are learned because they are followed by punishment. If your child's behavior indicates he is not responding to a "Don't signal," you will have to teach him what it means by following it with a punishing consequence.

Principle 5: Punish immediately, when possible.

Just as immediate reinforcement is more effective, so is immediate punishment. If a delay is allowed, it may not be clear that the behavior you want punished will be the one affected. As we also pointed out in discussing reinforcers, delayed punishment can be made effective with verbal children by carefully describing the behavior that brought on the punishment. This leads to a final principle:

Principle 6: Tell your child exactly what you are punishing him for and do it in a calm way.

Just as praise of specific behavior is more likely to teach a child what you want him to learn to do, so will being specific about the behavior you are punishing your child for help him learn what not to do. For example, such phrases as "You're a bad boy," "Mommy's mad at you," and "Don't do that," without specifying the "that" are inappropriate. More likely to be effective are these:

- "I am sending you to your room because you hit Jimmy."
- "You can't play with your cars today because you didn't put them away last night."
- "You have to come inside because you went out of the yard."
- "I'm fining you five points for getting out of bed."

WITHDRAWING REINFORCERS

There are two somewhat different punishment procedures involving the withdrawal of reinforcers. These are called *time–out* from positive reinforcement and *response cost*.

The essential ingredients of an effective time–out procedure are: (1) an ongoing reinforcing situation that the child does not want to lose (like being with mother, playing with friends, earning points); (2) a clear statement of what actions will lead to punishment by removal from the reinforcing situation; (3) one warning, and (4) actual placement in a time–out area. At home, most often a time–out area is a bedroom from which toys have been removed, such as Rorey's mother used. In using time–out, the parent should specify the conditions that will end time–out. For example, "When you are quiet for two minutes, you can rejoin the family," or "I will come and get you after you have been quiet for two minutes." The objective is to make the end of time–out a reinforcer for "good" behavior, just as the start of time–out was used to punish unwanted behavior. Time–out is often used for behavior problems usually maintained by parental attention such as tantrums, negativism, and disobedience.

Response cost involves taking away specified amounts of specified reinforcers. A child can lose points, tokens, or other credits earned toward future reinforcers, or he can lose time in desired activities, or he can lose actual treats of various kinds. To be effective, it is necessary to have: (1) an ongoing reinforcing system that is valuable to the child, (2) a clear statement of how much the fines are and for what behaviors, and (3) consistent assessment of fines when the misbehavior occurs. An important rule to remember in keeping fines effective is this: Do not set up a system in which the child is likely to have negative points (owes you money). Be sure the child can earn enough, in relation to fines, that he stays ahead of zero. Once he is broke, there is nothing to lose.

Another kind of response cost procedure might be called punishment by natural consequences. Consider these examples:

- Jimmy leaves the door open so he is required to go back outside, close the door, and come in again, closing the door properly.
- Mike tracks mud in the hall so he is required to clean it up.
- Billy breaks a neighbor's window with his ball so he is required to earn the cost of the replacement by cutting the lawn.

When a child's misbehavior is of the kind that causes you to do more "work," turn it around so that the child has to do the "work." In the process, he will learn about effort involved in undoing some of the effects of his own behavior.

USE OF FINES BY THE WALKERS

In Chapter Three, we discussed the point system set up by the Walker family for George, Dollie, and Keith. They could earn points for various tasks, and they could lose points for failure to complete tasks and for such behaviors as bickering, teasing, and whining (see Table 2, Chapter 3). The effectiveness of the fines used by the Walker family was studied experimentally.[2] Figures 1, 2, and 3 show the outcomes of that study for George, Dollie, and Keith, respectively. Look over Figure 1 first. The horizontal axis represents time, going from April 16 (4/16) to July 19 (7/19). The vertical axis represents the number of times a day George showed bickering, bedtime horseplay, and teasing. For example, from the start of the study until the arrow (when the point system was started without fines) George showed bickering about five times a day. After the point system was started for responsibilities he still showed bickering about five times a day. The solid vertical line indicates when the fine was started. The institution of the fine for bickering reduced bickering to about once a day on the average. At later times, fines were instituted for bedtime horseplay and for teasing. Again, Figure 1 shows a remarkable reduction in misbehavior when the fines are imposed.

Figures 2 and 3 show similar outcomes for Dollie and Keith. In each case, the use of fines drastically reduced the misbehaviors. This study dramatically demonstrates that some kinds of punishment can be effectively used in the home by parents.

Keep in mind the following:

1. The Walkers had a working token system going before they introduced the fines. The focus was first on the positive.

2. Fines were clearly specified as to what behaviors led to what point losses.

3. The fines were applied every time a deviation occurred.

FIGURE 1. Effects of 10-point fines on George. The arrows indicate when the point system was started for daily tasks. The solid vertical line indicates when the fines were started. Mean number of oppositional and cooperative behaviors and their parental attention contingencies. Means are based on the behavior of five parent-child cases. All observations were made during 20-minute clinic playroom session, held once a week. (From Christophersen, p. 490)

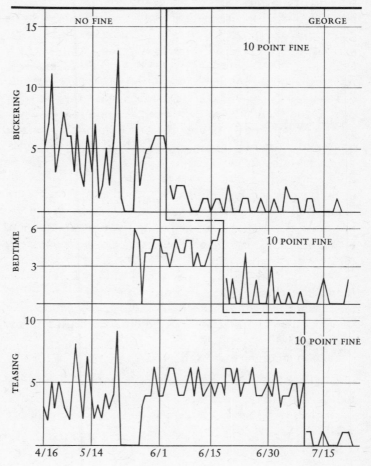

FIGURE 2. Effects of 10-point fines on Dollie. The arrows indicate when the point system was started for daily tasks. The solid vertical line indicates when the fines were started. (From Christophersen, p. 491)

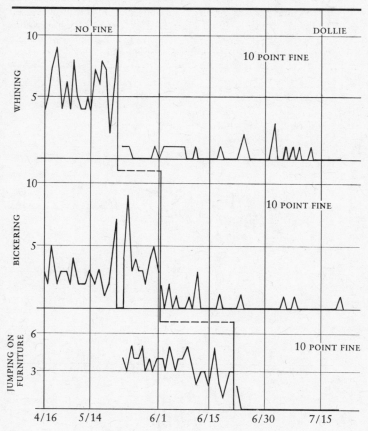

FIGURE 3. Effects of 10-point fines on Keith. The arrows indicate when the point system was started for daily tasks. The solid vertical line indicates when the fines were started. (From Christophersen, p. 492)

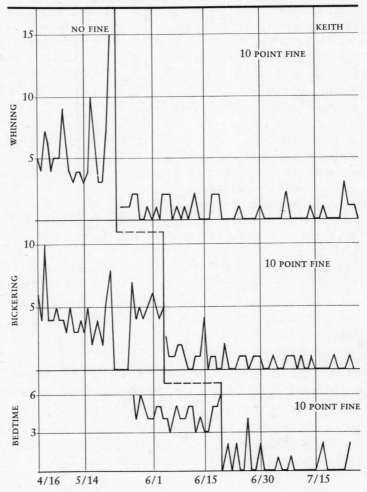

A Study of the Effects of Time–out

Wahler[3] studied five families with children who initially showed a high level of oppositional behavior. Oppositional behavior consisted of any failure to follow a request or command from parents. The parents initially were found to be giving a lot of attention to the oppositional behavior. To Wahler's surprise, removal of attention to oppositional behavior and training the parents to give praise and attention to cooperative behavior failed to change the children's behavior. As noted earlier, this procedure was found to be effective with many children, but it was not effective with these children. Figure 4 shows what happened. Under Phase 2, where attention is given only to cooperative behavior, there was no decrease in oppositional behavior. Furthermore, there was no increase in cooperative behavior. It was necessary to institute a punishment procedure in Phase 3 of the study before oppositional behavior decreased and cooperative behavior increased. The punishment consisted of isolating the children in their bedrooms for five minutes immediately after oppositional behavior occurred.

Further investigations by Wahler with other families confirmed the effectiveness of a combination of social reinforcement for cooperative behavior and time–out punishment for oppositional behavior. Wahler also made three more important observations that are consistent with the findings of other researchers:

1. When punishment for oppositional behavior was used consistently, the children started showing more positive approaches to parents.

2. The effectiveness of the parents' social reinforcers for their children was greatly enhanced following the use of time–out punishment.

3. The parents reported enjoying their children much more after the new program took effect.

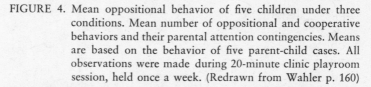

FIGURE 4. Mean oppositional behavior of five children under three conditions. Mean number of oppositional and cooperative behaviors and their parental attention contingencies. Means are based on the behavior of five parent-child cases. All observations were made during 20-minute clinic playroom session, held once a week. (Redrawn from Wahler p. 160)

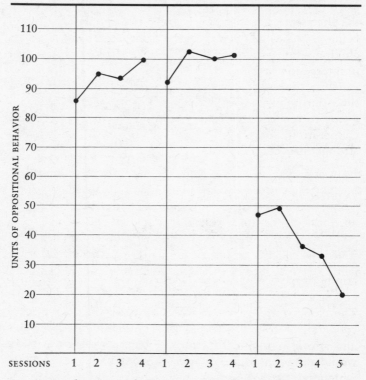

PHASE 1: Baseline Parental Attention to Oppositional Behavior

PHASE 2: Contingency Changes Parental Attention to Cooperative Behavior

PHASE 3: Contingency Changes Plus Punishment Parental Attention to Cooperation Behavior and Timeout for Oppositional Behavior

What could be going on here? First, it was necessary to suppress the oppositional behavior with punishment before there was enough cooperative behavior to reinforce. When a problem behavior is so frequent that you cannot find much incompatible behavior to reinforce, punishment may be needed to get a change process going. The children had to learn that their negative approach no longer paid off. Once the effects of punishment took hold, the parents could stop being grouches in a power conflict and begin to enjoy their children. Both the children and the parents like the new kind of interaction better.

These studies do not mean parents should always use a time–out punishment for oppositional behavior. Start with trying to reinforce an incompatible behavior (for example, cooperation) and only if this does not work, institute a stronger procedure.

FATHER LEARNS NOT TO USE "PUNISHMENT"

Mark was a seventh-grade boy who was referred to a behavioral clinic by a juvenile court.[4] He refused to do chores, was disobedient, and defiant. He destroyed toys and family property impulsively. He was stealing at both home and school. He had few friends and got into lots of fights. The clinic staff had much difficulty getting the parents to cooperate. Father handled all discipline with long lectures and strong whippings. Very often after a whipping Mark would destroy something, which became fuel for another whipping. Mark's mother tended to lecture him, but she never was very clear about her expectations of Mark. An allowance could be earned each nine weeks based on school grades.

Mark's parents were persuaded to try a new allowance system. Mark could earn a daily allowance of twenty-five cents if he showed no destructive behavior. If he did damage or destroy property, he lost the allowance and had to pay for the damages. Mark could also earn daily points for completing his chores and studying, which could earn him a bicycle in about six months. He very much wanted a bicycle. If Mark studied each day of the week, father was to give him a weekend bonus of an extra allowance or an outing with father. The parents kept daily records on Mark's behavior.

For seven weeks, progress was excellent. No destructive acts occurred, chores were rarely missed, and he studied daily. The parents were pleased but did not feel Mark should be "bribed" like that. They wanted to stop the plan. They were persuaded to continue, especially since his grades had improved too. Then a disaster occurred. Mark broke his glasses. This prevented a week of studying and infuriated father. Mark was punished, and the bicycle point-chart was stopped. In the next six weeks, although studying continued supported by praise from father, two minor acts of destructiveness occurred, as did some defiance toward mother. Completion of chores was dropping off. The parents decided that they had better return to the point system and the bicycle goal. A definite number of points was specified to earn the bike and Mark got it in thirty-four days with almost perfect behavior. His parents became believers in the value of making rewards contingent on desired behaviors.

The only punishment necessary to turn Mark from an "incorrigible," destructive delinquent was the potential loss of a daily reward. The remarkable change in Mark was accomplished largely through use of a positive approach. The moral is this: Even though some kinds of punishment work, a parent using a positive approach is not likely to need to use it except in rare circumstances.

TEENAGE PROBLEMS

Throughout history, parents have been told "Spare the rod and spoil the child." Punishment is assumed to be the key to

the teaching of good character. In the face of growing conflicts between parents and teenagers concerning the use of
drugs, sexual promiscuity, and other "crimes against the
establishment," many parents believe the solution has to lie
in punishment. As Claire's mother and Mark's father found,
punishing approaches are not likely to prove very effective
with teenagers. Teenagers can run away if parents get too
punishing. When that happens, all control is lost. One key to
the effective control of teenagers is to keep control over what
is reinforcing to them—free time, car keys, money, access to
friends—and be sure their behavior earns those reinforcers. A
second key is to know what your child is doing. Without that
you have no basis for responding with appropriate consequences. But the best solution is preventative. When parents
clearly know their values and teach them to their children
early, there is at least a chance when the temptations of early
adulthood must be faced. Chapter Ten is in part concerned
with the teaching of moral values through repeated examples and appropriate contingencies. But even more important
is building and maintaining strong bonds of love and respect
between parent and child. These bonds are most likely to
develop when parents give much love and affection to their
children but also judiciously punish undesired behavior following the rules presented in this chapter.

SUMMING UP

Punishment can be used to weaken undesired behaviors,
but it needs to be used sparingly and intelligently. When
physical punishment is used, it can generate fear or anger
toward the punisher and lead to avoidance and escape behavior. Avoidance and escape behavior lessen the parents'
opportunities to influence their child's development. There
are times of danger with young children, however, when the

directed use of punishment can efficiently teach about dangers.

Six principles for the use of punishment were presented:

1. Give reinforcement for behavior incompatible with the punished response.

2. Be sure the undesired behavior is no longer reinforced.

3. Generally punish by withdrawing reinforcers, rather than presenting painful events.

4. Use a "Don't signal" as a warning one time. If the warning is not heeded, back it up with an effective punisher.

5. Punish immediately, when possible.

6. Tell your child exactly what you are punishing him for, and do it in a calm way.

Two methods of punishing by withdrawing reinforcers are time–out and response cost. Time–out consists of isolating a child from all reinforcers for a specified period of time (two to five minutes). Response cost involves taking away points, money, or other reinforcers as a fine or penalty for misbehavior.

Even though punishment works, keep in mind that a positive approach comes first.

6 | *Basic Teaching Procedures*

Now that we know about consequences and some basic rules for using them, it is time to complete the picture of what teaching involves. Consequences can be used to make learning happen. The conditions under which the learning occurs are also important, however. The basic learning episode is a three step process:

SIGNAL $\longrightarrow$ BEHAVIOR $\longrightarrow$ CONSEQUENCE

The child learns to do, *under a given set of conditions,* that which is reinforced. The stimulus conditions or signal conditions under which learning occurs are every bit as important as what the child is doing. Signals are very important to intelligent behavior. Signals or cues help you know when to do what. Consider these examples:

SIGNAL $\longrightarrow$	BEHAVIOR $\longrightarrow$	CONSEQUENCE
• Red light.	Stop at curb.	Not get run over.
• Green light.	Cross street.	Get where you are going safely.
• "Come to dinner."	Go to the table and sit.	Eat.

• "Time to wake up."	Get up and dress for school.	Praise from mother. Breakfast.
• Dinner is over.	Do dishes.	Earn two points.
• "Please pass the potatoes."	Potatoes are passed.	"Thank you."

We teach signals by consistently reinforcing behavior that occurs in the presence of the signal. For example, to teach a child to say "Thank you" after you do something for him, you praise him for good manners when he does this, but do not praise him if he fails to say "Thank you." In this case, the signal is a helpful act by another, the behavior is "Thank you," and the consequence is praise. This example poses a basic problem parents must face in learning to be good teachers. What do you do if a child does not respond when the signal is present? How do you get the behavior to occur under the right signal conditions in the first place? There are two basic procedures for getting responses to occur to the proper signals. These teaching procedures are called *prompting* and *shaping*.

If the child can already make the response you want but does not make it to the right signal, prompting can be used to get the response going at the right time. In the example above, a prompt might be, "Say 'Thank you,' Mary." Mary can imitate what you say, so you tell her what to say. When she does it, you praise her for learning what to do to have good manners. Prompting uses signals a child has already learned about in order to get the same response to occur in a new situation.

If your child cannot make the response you want by using any tricks you know, *shaping* procedures must be used. Shaping involves a step-by-step building from some response your child can make to the new response. For example, if your child can suck milk from a bottle but not drink from a cup, the steps in a shaping program might involve step-by-step reinforcement of:

1. Child holding an empty cup.
2. Mother putting a swallow of milk in the cup and feeding it to her child, holding the cup herself.
3. Mother putting a swallow of milk in the cup and feeding it to her child, holding the child's hands and the cup.
4. Mother slowly reducing the help in holding hands and cup until the child can do it alone.
5. Mother adding milk to the cup in small amounts.

Note in this example, the milk will nicely serve as the reinforcer most of the time.

Shaping uses reinforcement of successive approximations to the goal. This is very much like the principle given in Chapter Three, namely, *reinforce improvement*. In shaping, however, the parent often has a carefully laid plan to follow in getting improvement.

USE OF PROMPTS

Any signal to which a child has previously learned to respond can be used to get that same behavior going under new conditions. Prompting signals include verbal instructions, words to imitate, signs, and a variety of special cues. Prompting can also involve physically moving your child through the response you want him to learn. Consider these examples:

- *Use of imitation.* You want your child to say "Bye-bye" when daddy leaves. Daddy starts to leave. You say, "Say 'Bye-bye' to daddy," and your child says "Bye-bye." Follow this with "You really did it!" or some such consequence.
- *A verbal reminder.* "You forgot to close the door."

- *Physical prompting*. Say, "Wave bye-bye," to your eighteen-month old and then take your child's hand and wave it at daddy.

There are two important principles to remember about using prompts:

Principle 1: Be sure the signal to which you want your child to learn to respond occurs *before* the prompt.

The signal, "Wave bye-bye" should occur before you help with the hand waving. This makes it possible in the future for the child to start to make the response on his own before the prompt is used. Similarly, the question "Who's coming home?" should precede your prompt "Daddy! Say 'Daddy'." Following this rule also saves you from just teaching your child to constantly look to you for prompts. If the signal he is to respond to comes first, it is more efficient for him to learn to respond to that signal rather than waiting for your prompt.

Principle 2. Fade out your extra help as soon as you can.

Fading involves a gradual withdrawal of your help. It can be accomplished in several ways. In physical prompting, you can gradually use less pressure in helping your child write his name. As your muscles work less, his work more. Verbal prompts can be made quieter (as in teaching to count), or shorter (you say, "it's a 'b' " rather than "it's a ball" in teaching your child the names of things). Special cues, such as signs, can be made smaller and harder to see, and so forth. The special help is faded as soon as possible so that the child learns to respond only to the signal you want him to learn about.

The following example illustrates the use of prompting within a program designed to teach a severely retarded girl how to imitate. The same kinds of procedures can be used to teach imitation to any young child. Imitating the behavior of another is a very important skill. With it, learning language through prompting can occur very quickly. Without it, language learning is next to impossible.

Susie was trained at mealtimes, with her food as the reinforcer. To train Susie to imitate, her teacher would give the signal, "Do this," and follow the signal with an action to be imitated. The first task was to raise her left arm. Susie did not respond to the signal, so her teacher raised her arm for her and gave her some food. After helping Susie make the response several times, the teacher began to fade his help as Susie began to respond on her own.

The next response to imitate was tapping the table with the left hand. When the teacher said "Do this" and tapped the table, Susie raised her hand. "Do this" was a signal to raise her hand, not tap the table. Again physical prompting was used to help Susie with the new "Do this." The teacher then went back to "Do this" and raising his hand. Susie tapped the table. For a series of trials, the teacher went back and forth between the two tasks (raise hand and tap the table) until Susie could do whichever one the teacher did. Then a new task was introduced. Each new task was learned more quickly and there was less confusion than with earlier tasks. After fifty tasks had been taught (over several months), Susie was imitating more than half of the new tasks the first time they were given. She was learning to imitate whatever her teacher did.

After Susie could imitate actions well, the teacher started on the imitation of sounds and words. This took a little work to get going because Susie had only been taught to imitate actions, not sounds. Her teacher finally got the first imitation of a sound by putting it on the end of a chain of action. He said, "Susie, do this." The teacher got up from his chair, walked to the center of the room, turned toward Susie, and said "Ah," and returned to his seat. Susie got up, went to the center of the room, faced the teacher, and began a series of facial and vocal responses out of which eventually came something close enough to "Ah" to merit reinforcement. The basis for teaching her to talk through imitation has been started.

Nagging. Some parents think they are prompting when

they give their children constant reminders about what they are supposed to be doing and not doing. This may be just a lot of nagging that keeps the unwanted behavior going. For example, mother "reminds" Linda for the third time that it is time to set the table without taking time to teach Linda to pay attention to the cues that suppertime is coming (food smells and the clock). Instead of saying repeatedly that "It's time to set the table," it might be more effective to ask Linda, "What time is it?" Or "Do you know what you are supposed to do?" This kind of prompting is more likely to get Linda responding to the cues she should be responding to than just telling her what she should do.

SHAPING PROCEDURES

Shaping is often needed in early motor skill development, including speech. In shaping, the parent uses reinforcers to build in a step-by-step way from what the child can do to a new behavior. The general steps are these:

STEPS	EXAMPLE
1. Define your objective.	I want him to tie his own shoes.
2. What behaviors do you have to build from?	He can imitate actions. He can grasp laces. He can make two hands work together.
3. Establish a reinforcer.	Maybe just being able to tie his shoes is enough. Maybe your praise is sufficient. Maybe points toward some treat needs to be given at each step to keep him motivated.
4. Specify the steps of your teaching program.	(See Figure 1)

FIGURE 1. Have a shoe with laces available for demonstration.
Use these procedures to tie the two laces.

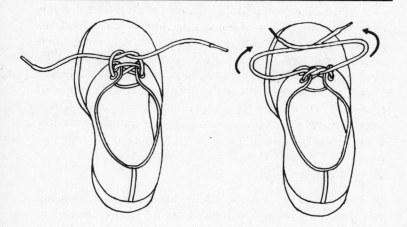

1. Make a half knot with the
   two laces.

2. Make a loop with the end of
   each of the laces.

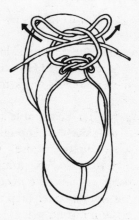

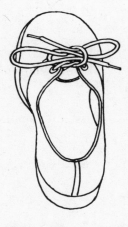

3. Make a second half knot
   with the two looped laces.

4. Pull ends of loops until tight.

The teaching steps are as follows: Place a shoe in front of the child, heel toward him. Sit beside him.

Step A. Go through steps 1, 2, 3, and 4 slowly to show your child it works.

Step B. Do steps 1, 2, and 3, and ask your child to pull them tight. "Good." Do it again.

Step C. Do steps 1 and 2 and have your child do step 3 with your help; he does 4 all alone. Repeat this until he can do steps 3 and 4 without your help.

Step D. Do step 1, then have your child do steps 2, 3, and 4, giving help on step 2 as needed.

Step E. Have child do step 1 with help; then he finishes 2, 3, and 4. Repeat until you are not needed. Praise along the way.

Step F. Have the child tie a shoe that is on his foot.

Step G. Check the procedure each day for the next week. If there is any trouble, go back to practice with a shoe placed in front of him.

NOTE: With a young child it may take more than one sitting to teach all the steps. Be patient. Don't go on to the next step until the previous step is done well. With a five-year-old this program should not take much more than thirty minutes.

5. Start training with the first step in the program.

You demonstrate with Step A and require the child to respond as in Step B.

6. Decide on the basis of your child's performance when to move on to the next step.

After two trials, your child could pull the laces tight. Move on. He will get more practice with that on each new step.

7. If after moving on your child fails the next step, return to the earlier success.

When you moved from the shoe in front of him to the shoe on his foot, he got mixed up. You return to Step E.

8. Repeat steps 6 and 7   He tied his shoes all by
   until the objective is   himself.
   reached.

In shaping, the parent has to know what the goal is and artfully reinforce improvements along the way. In this shaping program, the task was broken down into a series of simpler tasks and slowly put together. Note that we started at the end and worked backwards. The reason for this is discussed in the next section of this chapter. The procedure used is called backward chaining. Note also that the procedure gradually requires more and more of the child. You reinforce behavior that meets the new step requirements, and you no longer reinforce behavior that just meets earlier requirements unless you decide you have to go back.

Many applications of shaping procedures are contained in the discussions of early child care in Chapters Seven, Eight, and Nine. Shaping is often used in developing good eating habits, learning to play alone, learning to pay attention to tasks, learning to meet strangers, learning motor skills, and in learning speech. By using shaping procedures, we teach children without stress or unnecessary failure.

Parents should keep in mind the importance of shaping in teaching athletic skills. The skills involved in catching a ball, hitting a ball, throwing a ball, or making a basket do not come easy. They can be slowly built up at the same time you have fun with your child if you keep thinking of shaping procedures. Don't expect a six-year-old to have much fun with a ten-foot high basketball hoop and a full size ball. Start with a six-foot high basket and a volley ball, and raise the basket a foot each year until you get to ten feet. Switch balls when your child wants to switch.

CHAINING

The basic learning episode, SIGNAL–BEHAVIOR–CONSE-

QUENCE, can be extended into a chain of signals and behaviors such as this:

SIGNAL	See food
↓	↓
BEHAVIOR	Asks for food
↓	↓
SIGNAL	Food is passed
↓	↓
BEHAVIOR	Serves self
↓	↓
SIGNAL	Food on plate
↓	↓
BEHAVIOR	Puts food in mouth
↓	↓
CONSEQUENCE	Eats

Chains of behavior are established in most self-care skills, like learning to eat in a family-style setting. At first, you put the food on your child's plate and actually feed him. Next, he learns to get the food in his mouth. Once this is accomplished, you teach him to serve himself when you pass him food. Then, you teach him to ask for what he wants, to serve himself, and feed himself. Finally, you put into this chain appropriate considerations such as "Please" and "Thank you."

Behavior chains are stronger the closer you get to the reinforcing consequence. For this reason, it is easier to build from the reinforcer backward as we did in the shoe-tying example. By starting at the end, a tied shoe, the child is already successful. Then we go back one step, learn that, and we again have a tied shoe and success. By starting at the beginning, the chances of the chain breaking down are greater and so are the chances of failure. Language behavior can be built into longer chains by a similar process. "Go" becomes "Go store," which becomes "I want to go to the store." Getting ready for bed and for school are rather long chains that have to be gradually established by slowly requiring more of your child.

Why do chains stay together? It appears that what is happening is this: The signal for the behavior closest to the reinforcer becomes not only a signal, but also a reinforcer. New signals added to the chain also become reinforcers. We learned earlier that to make a neutral stimulus into a reinforcer, we follow it by a reinforcer and that's what happens in a chain. If the signals in a chain can also serve as reinforcers, then we have the glue to hold the chain together. Each behavior in the chain is followed by a reinforcer that is at the same time the signal for the next behavior in the chain. This is real technical stuff, so if you don't get it, just remember how to build chains. If you do it right, they will stay together, whether you know why or not.

A lot of chains with young children are initially established as interacting chains of behavior between mother and child. Chapters Seven and Eight are rich with examples of such chains. They take the form of I do this, you do that, I do this, you do that, and then the reinforcer. An example is the steps involved in getting your child into a high chair with bib on and ready to feed. Interaction chains are usually built in a forward direction. Consistent behavior by the parent is necessary to get them going. When a child is taught to care for himself, the patient's role is faded out of the chains and the child goes from one step to another on his own. For example, the bedtime routine of undressing your child, toileting, putting on night clothes, getting teddy and a blanket, bringing a glass of milk, and reading a story before tucking your child in slowly shifts from an interacting chain to a self-care chain in which your child gets ready for bed and you then read a story (or listen to one) and tuck him in.

SUMMING UP

The basic learning episode is a three-step sequence:

SIGNAL–BEHAVIOR–CONSEQUENCE. Signals help you know when to do what. We teach signals by consistently reinforcing the occurrence of the desired behavior in the presence of (or just after) the signal. Getting the desired behavior to occur in the presence of the signal is a basic teaching problem. Prompting and shaping are two teaching methods that can be used to get desired behavior going.

Prompting uses a signal to which children have previously learned to respond in order to get a response to occur to a new signal. Prompting may also involve just using your muscles to move your child through the response you want him to learn. Shaping is a procedure to use when there are no prompts you can use. Shaping involves a step-by-step building from some response your child can make to the new response. Shaping reinforces successive approximations to the desired behavior. Shaping reinforces improvement.

In using prompts, it is important to remember to first present the signal to which you want your child to learn to respond before you present the prompt. Fade the prompt as soon as you can. In shaping, it is important to know where you are starting from and where you are going so that you can establish the steps of your teaching program.

The basic learning episode can be extended into behavior chains by requiring additional SIGNAL–BEHAVIOR sequences to occur before reinforcement. Chains are often built by working backward from the reinforcer. This insures that there is adequate reinforcement for the new learning to occur. Interaction chains between parent and child are most common in the early training of a child. Over time, as the child is taught to care for himself, interaction chains are shifted to child behavior chains, as parental help is slowly faded.

7 | *A Happy Baby: The First Six Months*

Happy babies are "made" not born. The ways in which parents go about meeting their baby's needs have much to do with their baby's happiness. These needs are fairly limited at first. Your baby will need nourishment, warmth, freedom from discomfort, and activities to occupy him when he is not sleeping or receiving routine care. Care anticipates and avoids unpleasantness, provides essential supplies, and builds a sense of order and trust into your baby's life. Being a good parent is *giving* and *teaching*. Keep trying to teach your baby to take the next step, but stay ready to help if he fails to take that step.

The job facing the new parent is a difficult one, because there are so many uncertainties. Much of this uncertainty can be overcome by establishing a pattern of activities designed to meet your baby's needs. Two approaches have been commonly recommended in the past. The first uses a fixed time schedule to regulate the baby's life and meet his needs. In its strictest form, it is probably inadequate for individual infants, although it might fit the needs of some hypothetical "average" baby. In its more flexible forms, the schedule approach offers parents a rough guide for meeting the needs of their infant. The second commonly recommended approach is called a self-demand schedule. This schedule focuses on feeding, but can be thought of as applying to all the baby's activities. With this approach, your baby determines the schedule. An assumption underlying this approach is that the baby will make his needs clearly known and the parents will understand what is wanted. Unfortunately, there can be a great deal of uncertainty in interpreting an infant's needs.

A third way to look at the beginning job of caring for an infant is to see that it involves three things:

1. Learning to anticipate baby's needs.
2. Learning to read his signals.
3. Teaching him to read signals.

This approach is quite similar to the intent of a self-demand schedule. This reformulation, however, focuses more directly on what parents have to do and teach.

ANTICIPATING NEEDS

A time schedule can be a rough guide in anticipating needs. Some of your baby's needs do occur in time cycles. If he has just had a four-hour nap, it is unlikely that he is crying because he needs sleep. If he has just had cereal and four ounces of milk, it is unlikely that he is crying because he needs to eat. On the other hand, if he begins to fuss about three to four hours after the last feeding you can make a good guess that he wants to eat. The relation of needs to time patterns can be very helpful.

In addition to time patterns, you can use a checklist in searching for what to do. If your baby is crying and you don't know what to do, run through a checklist of possibilities such as this:

- Has he just waked in the middle of a sleep and simply needs to be left alone to return to sleep?
- Has he waked from a longer sleep and needs to be fed?
- Has he just been fed and needs to burp?
- Has he had the nipple removed from his mouth and his crying needs to be endured through a burp?
- Has he waked shortly after a feeding and needs water to help him return to sleep?
- Has he been on his tummy too long and would stop crying if you turned him on his back?
- Does he have a diaper rash that needs treatment?
- Does he need a diaper change?
- Does he need a change of scene?
- Is his head jammed into the corner of the crib?
- Is he crying during his sponge bath and would stop if you put a diaper over his tummy?
- Is he crying during his cereal feeding and would stop if you let him have milk between bites?

This kind of question-asking strategy is what you'll need to use to meet your baby's needs. In asking questions, consider food, diapers, temperature, sleep, gas, position, pain, physical restriction of movement, and boredom. If, after several minutes, you have tried everything that might be appropriate and your baby is still crying, don't get trapped into repeatedly trying a whole list of things. If you put him in his crib and leave him alone, chances are he will fall asleep in a few minutes.

READING YOUR BABY'S SIGNALS

It is not hard to tell when a baby is distressed. The trick is to try to learn what to do before he gets upset. Anticipating troubles will help greatly to avoid extreme distress. During this period you need to develop skills in reading less obvious signals than crying. The key to this is to pay attention to the sequences of behavior your baby shows, as they often contain very reliable signals. For example, activity may increase before your baby actually begins to cry for food. Maybe he tries to eat his fist when he's hungry. Maybe he flails his arms when his position is uncomfortable. Maybe he rubs his ears when he's tired and ready for sleep. Maybe he arches his back and stiffens when he needs a new position. Whatever his signals are—learn to read them by offering what you think he needs before he actually starts to cry. In this way you'll strengthen his output of clear signals and avoid teaching him a less clear and more upsetting signal system, namely crying.

This is an area that you and he will work on together for the rest of his growing–up years—how to give clear signals of needs. At first the work will seem to be all yours by learning to anticipate his needs and strengthen his signals. Later you will be involved in directly teaching him new signals to use. If a baby's needs are met as they occur, the behavior related to those needs will become predictable and provide you with clear signals. For a while it may seem that you will forever be a slave to your baby's stomach. But after four to six weeks there should be established routines for daily care that make life smoother for everyone involved. While routines must remain flexible according to your baby's needs, their development is critical to teaching your baby to read your signals.

TEACHING YOUR BABY TO READ SIGNALS

When you first begin caring for a newborn baby you realize how much you have to teach him. Literally nothing is a signal for him. Even the nipple in the mouth sometimes fails to quiet him for the first few seconds of a feeding. But over the weeks the nipple in the mouth becomes a signal that milk is coming, then the nipple near his face, then seeing the bottle in your hand, then seeing the bottle warming on the stove, then hearing your soothing voice, and so on until he responds to a wide range of signals associated with receiving milk. All these signals are taught to him by the consistent patterns you follow in routine care each day.

The basic procedure in this training is to use consistent sequences of behavior in interacting with your baby so that what happens *before* becomes a signal to what is coming next. For example, a typical sequence might be picking him up, putting him in his infant seat, tying on his bib, and then feeding him. As these actions are repeated, the early parts of the chain can have as quieting an effect on him as the feeding that comes at the end of the sequence. The cues associated with your various behaviors in the behavior chain come to be comforts because they are followed by a primary reinforcer (food). In addition to following consistent patterns of caretaking, be sure to use words, even at this young age, to describe what you are doing with him. At the least, he will come to pay attention to your voice and very likely begin to use your voice as a signal also. If you remain consistent in your sequences of caretaking, your baby will learn to read lots of cues you may not even know you are giving. Finally, make spaces in your sequences of caretaking to give your baby a chance to make responses. This will let you know he is reading your signals and beginning to build an interaction between the two of you.

During the first six months, parents teach children to read a wide range of signals. At first the only way you may know that your baby is reading them is that he cries less often and seems more relaxed during routine care. This is one way he can say, "I think I know what's coming next." Take diaper changing as an example. Diapering can be fun for you and the baby if you talk or sing while you change his diapers. You can talk about diapering, telling him what you're doing at each step. You can capture and hold your baby's attention with voice inflections, loudness changes, talking fast and then slow, and singing some parts. He will begin to "read" your actions and your voice by posture changes and body movements to cooperate with the diapering routine. You'll have to watch for his responses very carefully because they will be slight at first.

Other activities in which your baby will begin to read signals very early is in your picking him up, carrying him around, bathing him, and dressing him. The signals he reads will be sequences of your actions in handling and manipulating his body. His responses to these signals will be general relaxation and then gradually cooperation in the way he changes his posture or moves his head, arms, legs, and trunk. As in the diapering routine, these actions on his part may go unnoticed unless you are very attentive to his early attempts to read your signals and cooperate with you.

GOALS AND METHODS IN EARLY CARETAKING

The objective in this section is not to provide an exhaustive manual on how to rear a baby but to illustrate key principles and ways to avoid common problems. Essentially, the ideas presented are applications of the use of reinforcement principles with the very young baby.

FEEDING

The first six months is the time to establish patterns that can help to avoid eating problems in the future. Problem eaters are usually children who are resistant to eating a wide range of nutritious food and often make mealtime unpleasant for everyone by their balkiness. During this first six months, the variety of food you offer your baby expands greatly. He will probably be drinking milk, water, and fruit juices and eating cereal and a wide variety of fruits, vegetables, and meat by the time he reaches his six-month birthday. You will have many chances to teach him to enjoy eating a wide variety of foods.

Feeding time should be a pleasant time for you and your baby. It should be unhurried so that there is time to enjoy eating and enjoy each other. During the first few weeks it may seem that your baby hardly knows you are there, but if you start talking and singing to him, he'll begin to attend to your face and your voice.

Accepting solid food, usually cereal, will be your baby's first step in becoming a good eater. It would not be unusual for your baby to spit the cereal out of his mouth many times during the first several feedings. He's just learning how to deal with this new food experience. Simply scoop it off his chin and put it back in his mouth. You may have to do this dozens of times. Offering milk right after a small amount of cereal may help your baby adjust to his first solid foods.

If your baby shows resistance to solid foods, just remember that you can't win by trying to force him to eat. Try making the cereal thinner or thicker, try giving it to him faster or slower. Put more or less on the spoon and, as suggested earlier, try following each bite of cereal with a drink of milk. One of these suggestions may help your baby enjoy his cereal more. Your job is to teach your baby to enjoy his eating times. Trying to force him to eat this first solid food is not likely to help him enjoy it. If your baby is really resistant to cereal, it may be wise to stop offering it for several days. Maybe your pediatrician will suggest mixing fruit with the cereal when it's time to start fruits in your baby's diet. In any case, how early in life your baby accepts his first solid food is not very important. What is important is that you get him off to a good start in enjoying mealtimes.

As each new type of food is introduced into your baby's diet, you have a chance to teach him to accept and enjoy new foods. When introducing a new food, offer it at the mealtime when your baby is most eager for solid food. Offer only small bites at first. Alternate it with bites of something familiar that you know he will accept. Talk about the new food in the same way you describe and "recommend" the familiar and acceptable foods in his diet. Talk as if you assume and expect that he'll like what's coming, but don't make a big deal out of it.

If he's hesitant about new foods, don't be alarmed. He's telling you he can discriminate. You should be proud of him. Most likely, if you give him a little time and don't try to force him, he'll accept most of the new foods as they're offered.

If your baby really refuses a certain food, for example, squash or strained pork, simply stop offering it during that feeding and provide an acceptable substitute. You can then offer it again in a few days. He may accept it willingly the second time. If not, wait a few weeks to try it again. The principle is, don't try to force him to accept a particular food. If you force him, you'll lose and associate unpleasant feelings with eating.

As each new food is added, it should be less difficult to get your baby to accept and enjoy it. By the time he's six months old you have probably introduced a wide enough variety of foods to your baby that he should be well on his way to good eating habits.

Infancy is the time to avoid the pattern of offering food (including milk) as a comforter for any crying or upset that occurs. Feeding should be restricted to satisfying hunger, and not be a cure-all for his discomforts. Offering food to stop crying may seem to do the job, but (1) it has a temporary effect and may really increase the amount of crying in the future, and (2) it teaches the baby an unrealistic and incomplete method of dealing with his needs. If food is frequently offered as a comforter, it will reduce the chances of your being able to teach your baby how to express and deal with a wide range of needs. Not all crying is associated with hunger. He may be bored, fatigued, or uncomfortable.

This does not mean that an extra bottle should not be offered at possible stressful times. If, for instance, there is going to be a break in his routine and you expect that he may become upset, it is appropriate and helpful to give extra milk *before* he begins to cry. Suppose you are going to spend a day visiting relatives and expect that your baby may cry rather than fall asleep readily, as is his usual pattern. It might be very helpful for your baby to have a little warm milk just before he is settled down to sleep.

You could just put him down and ignore his crying and discomfort. That might work. But you might find yourself with a howling infant who is disturbing others and shows no sign of quieting. Then you're trapped into responding to a baby who has been crying vigorously for some time, and you risk teaching your baby that *strong* crying pays off. So you may find that a few ounces of warm milk is indeed just the thing to offer to a young baby who may experience an upset at a change of routine. Ideally, you offer the milk before the baby becomes intensely upset.

Being flexible parents, giving more comforts during times of stress, is appropriate all through your child's growing-up years.

SLEEPING

Your job in this area is to teach your baby to fall asleep alone in his crib. You can avoid a lot of bedtime problems if you never develop patterns of assisting your baby in falling asleep. The pattern of leaving your baby to fall asleep alone is easily begun when he is a newborn. Most likely he'll fall asleep easily with no attention from you soon after, if not during his feedings. It's then an easy matter to settle him in his bed and leave him alone. If he falls asleep before you get him to bed and he needs a burp or a diaper change, you'll probably wake him a bit to complete these tasks, but once settled in his bed he'll soon fall asleep.

Do not take these suggestions to mean you do not rock and cuddle your baby and otherwise show physical love. A rocking period can be made a part of a bedtime routine. The thing to avoid is teaching your baby that the only way to go to sleep is while being rocked. Rock him a while and then put him in bed before he goes to sleep. When you place him in his crib, you should leave him and let him fall asleep alone. If you're reading his signals appropriately, you should have no problems. Babies do not resist sleeping or require assistance in falling asleep unless taught to do so.

This advice does not mean that you never go to your baby if he is crying in his crib shortly after you put him down to sleep. This is not, however, the time to go to him *immediately* unless you can peek in at him without his detecting you. Wait several minutes. Quite likely he'll stop crying and fall asleep. If after several minutes he's still crying, go to him and see if you can determine the reason for his crying. Check out the possibilities and do whatever you think would be helpful in allowing him to fall asleep alone. Changing his position is probably the first thing to do. Don't plan to stay near him, pat him, or rock him until he goes to sleep. Once these patterns are begun, they are hard to break up.

Also note that teaching your baby to go to sleep on his own does not mean that you can put him in his crib at any time simply for your own convenience and expect him to fall asleep. It is your responsibility to read his fatigue signals and put him in his crib only when you believe he is ready for sleep. If you are fairly accurate in reading your baby's signals for sleep and if you have established a pattern of leaving him to go to sleep by himself, you are well on the way to avoiding bedtime problems with your baby.

Socializing

Your job in socializing your baby is to teach him to respond to a wide range of social behaviors in other people and to make a wide range of social responses himself. During the first six months your baby will change from a completely asocial being to a very sociable little creature. Your teaching will be responsible for this change. You will have made a substantial start in the long and exciting process of becoming an interesting human being.

As you begin to care for your newborn baby you will probably find yourself talking and singing to him, trying to get him to look at your face, holding and rocking him, and in other ways trying to capture his attention and get him to respond to you. This is exactly as it should be. You should begin making social responses to him right from the beginning. You'll soon be rewarded with an intent stare, his head turning when you speak, and then his first beautiful smile! He's letting you know he can respond to social behavior and not simply to milk, cereal, a warm crib, and other physical comforts. As he begins to attend to social behavior he will probably not discriminate one person from another. He will smile at many faces and turn his head when he hears most anyone's voice.

Even at this early age you should make social responses to your baby in an attempt to please him. Your smile, presence, touch, and voice will become important to him, and with these responses you can begin to establish an interaction with him. You teach him to smile by smiling when he smiles. You teach him to babble by talking to him or babbling like him when he babbles. You teach him to reach for you by reaching back when he does. You teach him to pay attention to people by being his main source of comfort. Soon your baby will come to recognize a certain number of people in his life, though maybe only a small number. This is a kind of signal-reading on his part. In a sense, he's saying, "Oh, I know you. You bring me warm milk, talk to me, smile at me, and come when I cry." Or, "I know you. You tickle me, bounce me, bring me toys, and make me laugh."

There are many opportunities in the routine of a day to play with your baby. At first he may be asleep except when receiving care, so you combine play and caretaking. You talk and sing to him during diapering, bathing, dressing, and feeding. While you talk and sing, try to "catch his eye," try to get him to look at your face. When he does look at your face, smile at him. Spend some of his awake times holding and rocking him. Teach him to feel comfortable and relaxed in your arms.

As he begins to be awake longer and is more alert you can spend more time in play sessions. You can begin to use toys and other objects to attract his attention. Soft squeaky toys are fun. He will begin to smile and soon laugh out loud when you squeak his toys.

Peek-a-boo will be fun for your baby too. He will learn to be very attentive to your face as it appears and disappears behind your hands and to listen carefully to your voice as it surprises him with "Peek-a-boo."

Songs, poems, and nursery rhymes are appropriate even before your baby understands any of the words. He'll listen attentively to your voice as it changes inflections, gets louder and softer, and pauses before the punch line. Even stories you make up about his daily life can be told while he's eating cereal or getting a diaper change.

Try saying his name to get his attention. If he turns toward you when you say his name, show him a toy or a picture. As this is repeated, he'll learn to respond by focusing his attention on you when you say his name.

As he begins to coo and babble, the two of you can begin to have "conversations." Give him plenty of time to "say his part" before you "answer" him. When you do answer you might try to imitate some of his more frequent sounds. This kind of conversing is the beginning of a true verbal interaction that will soon predominate his social life.

ENTERTAINMENT

As your baby passes three or four months of age, you may be tempted to say of him, "He's so bored. I can't seem to keep him entertained." That may be a fairly accurate description of his behavior. He will be awake several hours a day, but his mobility is strictly limited and his posture is strictly limiting. He can't move around much to keep the scene changing, and his skill and strength at sitting up (with and without assistance) is just developing. So he's trapped in space, so to speak. Also, his grasp is just developing. He'll have trouble grabbing, holding, and releasing objects.

Your job at this time is to provide as much of a variety of objects and events as will keep your baby alert and content.

His crib is one area of his life to focus on, since he will spend a lot of time there. His crib should be primarily a place for sleep. But your baby will not fall asleep instantly when placed in the crib and will probably not be removed from the crib instantly upon waking. He will spend some time awake in his crib and this time can be used effectively to teach him to deal with being alone.

It is entirely appropriate to make his crib interesting. Mobiles, cradle gyms, colorful bumper pads, music boxes, mirrors, and a wide variety of toys are available to decorate the crib. These need not all be displayed at once. In fact, your baby will probably give more attention to them if they are changed and cycled than if they are static and constant.

Different play areas are helpful at this time. A blanket on the floor with toys available will keep the baby entertained for short periods also. Cycling toys in these play areas is an effective way to keep the baby content.

Learning to sit up is a part of his work at this stage. You will need to assist in this by propping him in positions that strengthen his back muscles, holding him in a sitting position on your lap, bringing his infant seat into a more upright position, and perhaps tying him in his high chair or car seat for short periods. Getting him into an upright position allows him to see the world from a different perspective. This new position and perspective allows for a wider range of visual activities. The new position also puts his arms and hands into a more useful position for reaching toward and grasping objects.

You can encourage reaching and grasping in other ways too. Simply placing objects close to him will help. The objects will be easier to grasp if they are soft and have contours that fit his hand. A cradle gym in his crib or playpen will encourage reaching and grasping.

Encouraging movement and action is essential at this time. Make your baby's play area large enough to allow rolling over and over. Put toys out of his reach to encourage mobility, in whatever form it takes, toward an object. Even at this early age a Crawligator* may be appropriate for short times. Swings and jumping chairs are fun for a baby who is learning the effects of his own actions.

This is an appropriate stage to begin to think about and plan how to begin teaching your baby to play alone. This does not mean that you never play with him. You do spend lots of time playing with him. This is the way you socialize him. But there are times when it is appropriate for him to play alone. You can begin now, even at this very young age, to teach him to enjoy his time alone.

Let's suppose that your baby is awake and alert, has been fed and changed, and you must prepare dinner. Let's also suppose that you and your baby are alone in the house. This means that you cannot give your full attention to your baby and no one else is available to entertain him either. How can this situation be handled most pleasantly for you and your baby?

Leaving your baby alone in his playpen for the forty-five minutes it takes you to prepare dinner is not likely to work.

---

* A Crawligator is a molded platform on casters that supports the baby's body a few inches off the floor so that he can propel himself using his arms and legs. It is marketed by Creative Playthings.

Before too long he may be fussing, and if you let it go to strong crying, you're in trouble. To have a happy baby you need to anticipate. You don't wait until your baby is distressed to come to his aid. You anticipate possible distress and discomfort and alter this situation before your baby is upset. You might leave him in his crib five to ten minutes, return with some new toys, remove him from the crib after another ten minutes, hold him and talk to him a few minutes, put him in his swing in the doorway for several minutes, then put him in his infant seat near you. This may seem inefficient and demanding of your time and energy. Actually, quite the opposite is true. It is easier to avoid distress than to try to deal with it after it has occurred. And there is less wear and tear on both you and your baby. It is more pleasant to interact with a happy, alert, smiling baby than a baby who is crying and agitated. As the days and weeks go by, you can gradually extend the time he plays alone without your attention.

SUMMING UP

Happy babies develop when their parents learn to anticipate their needs, learn to read their signals, teach them to read signals, and generally teach them to cope with daily routines with a minimum of upsets through a thoughtful use of behavior principles. The more skillful parents become at anticipating needs, the less fussing and crying. The less fussing and crying, the less likely that fussing and crying will be learned as ways to get parental attention, and the more likely better ways to communicate will be learned.

Anticipating needs builds first on the cyclic nature of the baby's needs and then develops into a communication between parent and child based on signals given by the baby and read by the parent, or vice versa. The key in learning to read your baby's signals is to attend to the things he consistently does before he gets upset. His anticipatory movements and vocalizations are likely to contain consistent cues for parents as to what is coming. By establishing daily routines, your baby can learn to read signals. He will learn that relief from discomfort is coming long before it happens and thus be happier about waiting. Early routines also provide the chains of interactions upon which a true communication between parent and child is built.

8 | *A Happy Baby: Seven Months to Two Years*

Your baby will make fantastic changes in these eighteen months. He will become very mobile. He will become curious and eager to explore. He will begin self-feeding, first with his fingers and then with a spoon and fork. He will learn to drink from a cup and then to hold his own cup. He will be very sociable and enjoy being near people, but he may be shy with strangers. He will begin to really play with his toys in an inventive way. He may begin, but may not achieve, toilet training. He will begin imitating sounds and words, using single words and perhaps even sentences. He will certainly understand a great deal of what you say to him. In short, he will change from a helpless infant to a capable young child.

Your job during these eighteen months changes too. You will still be involved in meeting needs, anticipating those needs, reading your baby's signals, and teaching him to read other people's signals. Your focus, however, will change and you will be spending less time and energy simply meeting and anticipating those needs and more time teaching your baby to give clear signals and to read other people's signals.

You will begin teaching him to become a cooperative member of a group (family, friends, peers) rather than just a receiving member. He will by no means fully achieve this cooperative status. You will be involved in teaching independence and cooperation during all his growing–up years.

EXPLORATION AND MOBILITY

During the first twenty-four months your baby will master rolling, crawling, creeping, pulling up, walking alone, climbing, and running. He may also learn to move about on a Crawligator, walker, or scooter if he has the opportunity. He will be very curious and eager to explore. Even before he is mobile, he will be grabbing everything he can reach.

Your job will be a dual one. As he begins to move and explore, provide an environment that allows and encourages maximum mobility and exploration with plenty of safety and few frustrations. Then gradually teach your baby to watch out for his own safety, anticipate and avoid his own frustrations, and abide by rules to safeguard the rights of others while he moves about and explores.

Providing an encouraging, safe, nonfrustrating environment is your first job. When your baby begins to move around a little, a playpen may be appropriate. A blanket or rug on the floor may do just as well. To encourage your baby to move out and explore, you can put some toys out of his reach. You should check him often to see that he hasn't moved into a dangerous situation (electrical outlet, stairs, small objects he could swallow). At this point in his development, a Crawligator may encourage movement and exploration.

As he achieves crawling (tummy on the floor) and creeping (tummy up), he will begin to move more quickly and a blanket on the floor will not contain him. A playpen or a portable gate might be used to keep him in the room you're in so that you can keep an eye on him as he explores his growing environment.

A walker broadly expands the area to be explored. As he learns to "drive" his walker, he comes in contact with objects he could not see or touch from the floor. Now you can put toys on chairs and tables to encourage active exploration. You are probably wise to remove things from his reach that are not for his use.

"No-No"

As your baby pulls up, stands, and then walks, he will have the skills necessary to "get into everything." This is the time to begin teaching him the limits and rules of moving about and exploring. The environment should still remain safe, encouraging, and relatively nonfrustrating. It is not practical, however, to attempt to structure and control the entire house and all its members to fit your baby's wishes. You will be involved in teaching your baby "No-no."

His first "No-no" lessons will probably be "Don't touch that object." If your baby walks at a very young age, it may take more time to teach him this first "No-no" lesson than if he is a relatively late walker. How long it takes him to learn what "No-no" means is not very important. It is important that he learns: (1) that when you say "No-no" you mean it, (2) that what was a "No-no" yesterday is still a "No-no" today, and (3) that when something is forbidden he should look for something to do that is not forbidden.

There is no place for anger in this first "No-no" lesson. Forbidding things and activities is not an angry act. You are simply teaching your baby that some things are for his use and some things are not. You should be matter-of-fact in teaching this lesson. The fact that you are discouraging or eliminating some of his behavior and are therefore involved in a punishment process does not necessitate anger. If done correctly, it will not cause particular stress for either of you.

When you first begin to encounter a need to teach "No-no" (that is, when he is active enough to "get into everything"), you should use a type of distraction method. If your baby approaches, touches, or grabs something he is not allowed to handle, go to him, say, "No-no," remove the object from his hands if necessary, take him to something that is allowed, and say, "You can play with this." The fewer different things he has to learn "No-no" about at the start, the better. Maybe two or three forbidden things are appropriate to start with.

After several times of physically interrupting him while saying a "No-no," try saying "No-no" *just before* he starts to grab a forbidden object. If he does stop, go to him immediately, say something to let him know you are pleased, take him to something that is allowed, and say, "You can play with this."

Later try simply saying "No-no," praising him when he follows your instructions, and then letting him find a more suitable activity on his own. You might be able to help him by pointing out or suggesting a toy. Soon he will learn to avoid the forbidden objects without your reminders and to play with and explore those objects you do not expressly forbid.

When he has learned the "No-no" lesson about a few objects, it's time to expand to additional forbidden objects. He will learn more quickly as time goes on. Soon he will begin to anticipate which things in the environment are for his use and which are not. He will probably even begin to ask if he can handle objects if you are pleasant and will help him find something suitable when you must say "No."

There will undoubtedly be times when a "No-no" warning does not work. You will say, firmly and pleasantly, "No-no," and your baby will disregard your warning and pick up some object you have forbidden. If you change your tone and repeat "No-no" in a harsh, loud voice, you will start a pattern of screeching at your baby. This pattern can be very unpleasant for anyone involved or present. You can make "No-no" an effective warning without voicing it in an angry way.

If you are in the very early stages of training and your baby is just beginning to learn what "No-no" means, you can expect errors, and you simply repeat the distraction methods suggested above. If, however, your baby has been responding to your "No-no" warning and then begins testing you, your job is to show him that when you say "No-no" you mean it. So if you give a warning he disregards, go to him, remove the object from his hands, repeat "No-no" in a firm and pleasant voice, give his hand a quick slap, then take him to something suitable, and say, "You may play with this."

You see that the steps are exactly the same as in early training except that you add a quick slap *just after* your "No-no" warning. You are teaching him that the warning is real. He can avoid the slap if he heeds your warning. Your warning should not change. You want him to learn that a firm, pleasant "No-no" is to be obeyed. If you only slap his hand after a harsh, loud, "No-no," you should not be surprised that he does not heed a more pleasant "No-no." If you follow these steps to strengthen your warning signal, you will probably find that you seldom need to slap his hands. An occasional reminding slap will be all that is necessary. An occasional slap is certainly preferable to a constantly escalating, screechy "No-no."

FRUSTRATION CRYING

Even though you have tried not to reinforce crying during the early months, and you may have very little crying as signals of basic needs, there will still be some crying. At this stage of increasing movement and exploration, there will undoubtedly be some frustration crying. It will occur when your baby is unable to complete some action he has begun. For example, he's started pulling up to the coffee table and is in a position of being unable to get either up or down; or he's started under a chair to reach a toy and gets stuck; or he's on his way in his walker and gets hung up on a rug. He will get into difficulty as he's learning to move about and explore. When he's frustrated, you can teach him some important lessons by the way you respond. If you are calm and matter-of-factly confident that you can help set his world straight again, you teach him that problems can be solved. Your job, again, is to avoid his getting into a pattern of crying as a signal to you. You should immediately go to him and matter-of-factly help him in his objective.

When your baby is thwarted in some objective and begins to fuss or cry, go to him, say, "I see you're having trouble," and give the minimum amount of assistance that will allow him to complete his objective himself. Don't solve the entire problem for him. Just straighten out, adjust, or remove the obstacle and let him proceed on his own. Or demonstrate a possible solution and see if he will try to imitate you. As you assist him or demonstrate a solution, describe what you are doing. "Let's see you go around the hassock." "I can put the *little* block on the *big* block." "Maybe you could pull the handle this way." "Let's try to back your scooter out of this corner." "Hold the box with your knees and then pull on the lid here."

You are trying to teach your baby several things. By going to him quickly you are teaching him that it's okay with you if he needs your help. You are teaching him an alternative to crying and fussing by saying, "I see you're having trouble." As he gets more verbal, you'll be able to teach him directly to say "trouble," "having trouble," or some verbal signal rather than fussing. And finally you are involved in teaching him that problems have solutions and he can learn to solve problems effectively.

CRYING WHEN HURT

As your baby is learning to move around, he's going to take some spills, and bumps and bangs do hurt. How you handle his reaction to these falls is important in teaching him about another kind of crying. Crying when hurt is legitimate and is a socially conventional way of signaling a need for comfort, but a balance must be taught. It is not appropriate to cry over every little bump and scrape nor is it healthy to never ask for comfort when hurt.

There is a way to distinguish between "real hurts" and "imaginary or little hurts." A "real hurt" leads to immediate, strong crying that diminishes with time regardless of whether comfort is provided or not. On the other hand, an "imaginary or little hurt" leads to no crying or mild crying that increases if you are present but do not provide comfort or pay attention. Your baby may not cry if alone or if comfort is not obviously available. Crying over "little hurts" is usually to get your attention.

Childhood is filled with falls, bumps, and scrapes, and the crybaby has a hard time living in this world. You'll do your baby a great service by teaching him early not to cry over "little hurts."

If your baby is really hurt and crying strongly, go to him immediately. Check him quickly for hurts that need treatment. If no treatment is appropriate, then comfort is what you have to offer. Let him know by holding him and telling him that you acknowledge and sympathize with his condition. "I'll bet that really hurt. You took a nasty fall." "I'm sorry you pinched your finger. I wish I could make it feel better." "Here, let me kiss your arm. It will be better in a minute." "It's too bad you got hurt. I'll hold you on my lap until you feel better."

If your baby is slightly hurt or startled by a fall or bump, you may not need to attend to him immediately. He may recover quickly on his own and continue with his activities. In this case, you need do nothing. If he shows signs of being about to cry, go to him and suggest or initiate something that will handle or distract him from his minor discomfort. "Oops. Jump up." "Look. Rub your head like this." "That was a little hurt. No crying." "Oh, that silly ole trike. See if you can make it go again." "I'm sorry you burned your tongue on those hot potatoes. Take a quick drink of cool milk and it will soon feel better." He will learn not to cry over "little hurts," and you'll seldom find it necessary to remind him to handle it himself.

Motor Skills

Chapter Nine will give specific teaching strategies to improve your baby's motor skills. However, interacting with an encouraging, safe, and nonfrustrating environment will do a great deal to teach your baby the limits of his mobility and exploration. It will also show him how to handle frustration and hurts. He will have the setting and opportunity to develop his motor skills as he moves and explores.

FEEDING

Your job is still to teach your baby to enjoy eating nourishing food. During the first two to three years of his life, you will have fairly good control of what food is available to your baby and when it is offered. When he begins to move about "alone" in the larger world of babysitters, nursery school, friends, and relatives, you'll have less control of his eating. Therefore, you should use the early years to establish good eating habits.

New Foods

As your baby passes into the second six months of his first year, he will move from strained baby food to chopped food and some table food. Your pediatrician may suggest diet changes as he thinks they are appropriate. Remember that when you do add new foods or change to a new texture and consistency, the sensation will be unfamiliar to your baby. He may show momentary hesitation or he may really balk. If he does balk at a new food, simply substitute another food that is familiar and acceptable, and then offer the new food again soon. If he again refuses, wait a longer period before trying again. If he refuses a new textured food, you might see if he would eat it if it were more similar to the texture he is used to. For example, if he refuses chopped carrots, see if he will eat them mashed. Or if he balks at one of the commercial toddler dinners, see if he might accept it if it were mixed with one of his favorite strained vegetables. The idea is to help him move on to more grown-up foods in whatever size steps are acceptable to him. This is a shaping process.

As your baby begins to feed himself, he will begin joining the family for meals and eating some of the things that are served there. If he is using his fingers to feed himself, his food should be in pieces he can pick up easily. This includes chopped meat, many vegetables, most fruits, bread, hard-boiled egg, cheese, crackers, Jello, macaroni. At this time there's no reason to give him cake, cookies, candy, and other rich or sweetened food. If you let him expand his food preference within the range of meats, vegetables, fruits, cereals, and dairy products before you begin to offer desserts, he is more likely to accept these more nourishing, but perhaps less "tasty," foods.

When he is feeding himself, he still may balk at a new food. He will be able to recognize new foods even before he tries them. They will *look* unfamiliar. Don't ask him if he wants to try the new foods. If he says "No," you're trapped —you should abide by his answer because you asked, but you want him to try the new food. Simply put some of the new food on his plate and invite him to try it. Try to be unconcerned about whether he eats it or not. If he does not try some during the entire meal, remove his plate when he's done and don't comment. If he tried a little bit and then didn't finish it, quietly say, "I'm glad you tried a little bit of this macaroni." If he ate all that you gave him, give him a little more, saying, "I see that you really like this new macaroni. It has a good taste, doesn't it?" The point is that you should not force your baby to eat what he doesn't want. As long as you provide nourishing food for him to choose from and offer quantities that are sufficient to satisfy him, that is the best you can do.

SNACKS

In addition to controlling *what* food is available, you also control *when* food is available. In most households, the most nourishing food is served at mealtimes—the snacks may include foods of questionable nutrition. If you allow your baby to indulge in indiscriminate snacking, you may find that he is seldom very hungry at mealtimes and consequently eats only small portions. However, since your baby will not immediately accommodate himself to three meals a day, you will need to provide small snacks between meals for awhile. These snacks should be nourishing but not too filling. Fruit, raw vegetables, cheese, crackers, and cereal bits make good snacks. If the snack is offered close to a coming meal, your baby should be given a limited amount and not allowed to eat as much as he wants. He could spoil his appetite.

When your baby begins to feel comfortable on three meals a day, there will still be times when snacking is appropriate. This will be particularly true if a meal is going to be very late. A small snack can keep your baby from getting fussy and irritable. Another occasion when a snack may be appropriate is when a previous meal has not provided a satisfying quantity and choice. Perhaps you visited a friend for lunch and the choices of food available were simply not appropriate for your baby. It would then be wise to offer a snack (or another lunch) before putting him down for a nap.

Change in Appetite

As your baby passes his first birthday, you may notice a change in his appetite. He may begin to eat less. It is reasonable that he should do so. The rate of growth during the second year is far less than during the first year, and he is utilizing his food better. If he eats less than you think he should, remember you cannot force your baby to eat. If you get upset and give your baby lots of attention for refusing food or try to coax him to eat by offering a tasty dessert, he'll soon learn that not eating leads to a payoff, and you'll be teaching poor habits. The general rule is—when your baby does not eat all you think he should, remain noncommittal and simply remove his plate. He'll probably eat more at the next meal.

Feeding Himself

As your baby starts to learn to use a spoon, fork, and cup, he'll very likely be messy for awhile. Your job is to give him time to master these skills and not focus on the mess. You could dampen his enjoyment of mealtimes if you're constantly criticizing him about spills. Since food tastes better in his mouth than on the table, the floor, or his bib, he'll have a built-in consequence for getting the food into his mouth. You can compliment him for getting it there and show him you are pleased with his improvement. You can also give him food that sticks on the spoon when he's first trying to manage that tool. When he begins to handle his own cup, it is very helpful if you put in only as much fluid as he can take in one swallow. He'll learn to tip the cup up long before he learns when to lower it. You can save lots of spills and sputtering if you don't overfill the cup. Just have a container available at the table from which to refill his cup with one swallow.

BEDTIME

If you did your job well during the first six months, your baby should easily fall asleep alone in his crib. You should continue to expect that he will do this. His sleep habits will change, however, and there will be times when you think it's time for sleep, but he may resist being put to bed. These times will most likely occur when he is ready to eliminate one of his naps or stay up a little later in the evening.

Keeping Bedtime Positive

Being put to bed should not be used as a punishment. Nor should bedtime be presented as unpleasant. It should be considered just as pleasant as mealtimes and playtimes. There's a world of difference between saying "You have to go to bed now," and "You get to go to bed now." Admittedly, this small verbal difference will be lost on your baby, but your attitudes about bedtime will come through in many ways whether you think of bedtime as a "have to" or "get to." If you think of bedtime as a "have to," you are probably not responding to your baby's signals about his very real need for sleep. You may be responding to a clock, to some fixed notion of how much sleep a baby needs, or to your own convenience and need for time away from your baby. Whatever makes you consider your baby's bedtime a "have to," try to change your attitude. Your baby will inevitably pick it up and most likely become resistant. You will not be in tune with his needs and he'll know it.

If you read your baby's fatigue signals correctly, present bedtime as a pleasant activity, and establish some enjoyable pre-bedtime routines, your baby will seldom resist being put to bed. For example, if you see that your baby is sleepy, you might say, "Let's go see your teddy bear and your bed and you can have a nice nap." While you're getting him ready (removing shoes, putting on a fresh diaper, and so forth), you could sing a song he really likes or tell him a story about himself or recite a nursery rhyme. As your baby gets older, he can participate in some of the songs and stories. Then it can be fun to review the day. For example, as you are getting his pajamas on, you could say, "Let's see, what did you do today? Remember?" He may give you some activities. If he doesn't, you can suggest one and ask him if he remembers. He may then repeat what you said or may add something that he remembers about the event. Later it will be fun to anticipate the next day. Hugs and kisses may be added to close the interaction and leave your baby to fall asleep alone.

SECURITY OBJECTS

If your baby has a favorite bedtime toy, a security blanket, a pacifier, or a bottle, or if he sucks his thumb, he will probably have little trouble falling asleep, even in strange settings. For him, these props will be a very important part of his falling asleep routine. Once these habits build up they may be stressful to break, particularly after age eighteen months or so. If you feel that your baby should not have a pacifier, for example, it would be easier to eliminate it from his bedtime routine before age one. If his personal bedtime props are not offensive to you and not harmful to your baby, you may decide to let them persist until he gives them up on his own. There is no hard and fast rule about when children should abandon their "babyish" bedtime ways.

WARNING SIGNALS

As your baby gets older, you will need to give him signals that bedtime is approaching rather than beginning the routine without warning. When he is busy playing, being interrupted can be very frustrating. He may know that his bedtime routine begins when Daniel Boone is over on TV. But if there is not some clear signal in his schedule, you'll need to give a warning. Give him a few minutes to wind things up. You might say, "When you finish putting all your people in the bus, it will be time to start your bubble bath." Or you could say, "Ride your tricycle into your room and park it; and then you can jump into bed, see your Pooh Bear, and have a nice nap." Give him a chance to complete his play and provide a signal that bedtime and some part of it he enjoys are approaching.

BABY-SITTERS

Sometimes you will not be around when your baby goes to bed. Someone else, perhaps a relative or baby-sitter, will be putting him to bed. To avoid resistance and distress you should leave instructions about your child's bedtime routine. If he always has a drink, if you leave his night light on, if he has his door closed, or if he has a special toy or blanket, the baby-sitter should know these things. It is probably less important that she try to substitute for you in whatever interaction (songs, stories, hugs, and kisses) you and your baby have built into the bedtime routine.

RESISTANCE TO BEDTIME

If your baby cries after you put him to bed or shows resistance during any part of the bedtime routine, examine the way you are handling him and see if you are teaching him to cry and resist. Are you going to him if he fusses after you leave him and taking him an extra bottle, a drink, or getting him up? Are you teaching him to fuss and cry rather than fall asleep? Are you postponing the bedtime routine or adding extra activities to prolong it if he resists getting ready for bed? Are you teaching him to balk and resist? If you are, the solution is to stop responding to his crying and resistance, proceed with his bedtime routine, and leave him alone to fall asleep. You should remain matter-of-fact and ignore his fussing and crying. Crying and resistance will disappear in a few days if it does not pay off.

TOILET TRAINING

Toilet training involves teaching your baby to use a potty chair or toilet and then teaching him to tell you when he needs to use it. These are the two main skills your baby will learn during what is usually considered toilet training. Later he will also need to be taught to use toilets different from his own, to "wait" when no toilet is available, to tell other people besides you that he needs to "potty," to take himself to the toilet, and to stay dry while sleeping. These later tasks are not described in this chapter.

The age at which you begin or complete toilet training is not important, except perhaps as points of information for the baby book. How long it takes to complete toilet training and how many mistakes your baby makes are not particularly important either. What is important is that you and your baby complete toilet training in a cooperative and friendly manner.

While there are many opinions about when to begin toilet training, there is one general rule that may be useful to individual mothers. *The earlier you begin, the more time it will take to complete toilet training.* Of course, this rule is true only within reasonable limits. It might not hold true if you wait until your child is four and a half years old to begin toilet training. Also, remember the rule applies to actual time elapsed from beginning to completion of toilet training. It does not state that the earlier you begin, the later you will finish. For example, one mother might institute toilet training with her baby at fourteen months and finish at twenty months, taking a total of six months training time. Another mother might begin at nineteen months and finish at twenty-two months, taking three months. So the first mother-child team achieved toilet training at a younger age than the second team, although the second team worked at it a shorter time. You have to decide whether the extra work of earlier training is worth it to you.

In any case, sometime between his twelfth- and thirtieth-month's birthday your baby may start to give you signals that he is ready to begin toilet training. His diaper may still be dry after two or three hours; he may indicate he wants his diaper changed as soon as it is wet or soiled; or he may pull at his diaper. If he shows any of these signs or any other signs that suggest to you that he is aware of his toileting behavior, you could begin a trial toilet training period.

Whenever you begin, you should consider this beginning a trial. If you've made a mistake in timing or you make a mistake in procedure and your baby becomes upset, resistant, or balky, the best thing to do is postpone training for a few weeks. Nothing will be lost and a great deal may be gained. This does not mean that you quit at the first little sign of resistance. There may be some resistance as a result of the restriction on movement that sitting on the potty necessarily involves. The procedure described below is designed to handle this type of resistance.

TEACHING USE OF THE TOILET

When you begin, you need a potty chair and some training pants. A potty chair that does not tip easily and need not be attached to the toilet is preferable, since the baby can get on and off by himself. Place the potty chair in an area where the baby is free from distractions and interruptions.

You might also find it helpful to keep two charts, such as the ones that follow with sample data included.

FIGURE 1.

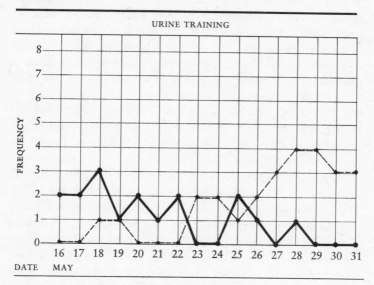

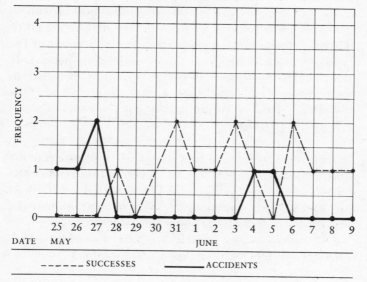

These charts are for your own information only. They can keep you objective and on target about your baby's changing behavior. These charts are only used for toileting behavior that occurs during those parts of the day when training is involved (that is, when the baby is wearing training pants), and not for toileting behavior that occurs when the baby is wearing diapers during the night, for naps, and for outings.

When you are ready to begin, dress your baby in his new training pants and clothing which are easy for you to handle when you take him to the potty. At this time you should say something like, "See your new pants? Let's see if you can keep these pants clean and dry."

After a few minutes, sit your baby on the potty and say something like, "This is where you are going to potty. See if you can potty now." If he tries to get up, sit him down gently. Keep him there no more than five minutes. A minute might be the most you can achieve the first few times. If your baby urinates or has a bowel movement, say something like, "You did a good job. You know where to potty." Most likely, nothing will happen and you'll say something like, "That was good sitting." Let him continue with his regular routine for about thirty minutes, commenting to him that you are glad his new pants are still clean and dry. Then bring him back to the potty chair and repeat the procedure. Continue in this way until your baby begins to use the potty chair. It might be helpful during active training to increase your child's fluid intake to increase the chances of success.

If you have trouble getting your baby to sit on the potty chair at all or in keeping him there for about four or five minutes, try this. Bring a short table, stool, or hassock next to his potty chair and put some crackers, cereal bits, cookies, marshmallows, raw potato slices, or carrot sticks there for him to nibble on while he sits. This bait will be necessary only until he gets the idea of what he's supposed to do. Once he begins to be successful in toileting he will not need to sit long and thus will not need goodies to hold him there. If he's been sitting on the potty at least six times a day for a week, munching away each time, and you have increased fluid intake and still there has been no toileting success, you'd better postpone toilet training for a few weeks. You may teach him that sitting on the potty is for eating snacks.

As your baby begins to use the potty, you can reduce the number of times you sit him on the potty. He'll gradually learn to wait for two to three hours at a time. If he's still having lots of accidents, increase the number of times you put him on the potty. You will begin to discover a schedule that fits his needs.

Your baby will have accidents. In fact, he may have more accidents than successes for the first few days or weeks. Punishment or criticism is not helpful in reducing the number of accidents. When he has an accident, even if he just got up from the potty, matter-of-factly clean up and get him dry pants. You should say something like, "You wet your pants. Let's see if you can keep these pants clean and dry." Don't scold. Don't try to make him feel bad. Just acknowledge that he made a mistake, and let him know you believe he'll do better next time.

TELLING YOU "POTTY"

When your baby has been using the potty successfully and has few accidents (maybe one every three to four days) for at least a month, you can start teaching him to tell you when he needs to use the potty. By this time you and your baby may have established separate words for urinating and having a bowel movement. Whatever word or words you use, you first begin by teaching your baby to say these words and teaching him what they refer to. Let's suppose you use "potty" for both actions. When you take him to his potty chair say, "It's time to potty. What is it time to do? Say 'potty'." When he says "Potty," you say, "Good, it is time to potty." When he has finished, say, "What did you do?

Say 'potty'." Continue this routine, dropping out the "Say 'potty' " prompt until he can answer both questions. If he can answer both questions, you can be sure he can (1) say the word, and (2) know to what the word refers.

By now you should have a fairly good idea of how often your baby uses the potty and have probably established a schedule that fits your baby's needs. You begin teaching him to tell you when he needs to go by helping him to anticipate going to the potty at farther distances from the potty chair, from different places in the house, and at various times. Each time before you actually take him near the potty, whisper in his ear, "It's time to potty," then say aloud, "What is it time to do?" If he says, "Potty," say, "You can tell me when it's time to potty," and take him to the potty. If he doesn't say "Potty," repeat the whole routine, adding, "Say 'potty'," and then take him to the potty. After a few days, stop whispering in his ear. Simply say, "What is it time to do?" If he doesn't say "Potty," whisper in his ear again. Keep trying to drop out the whispered signal until he can answer the question, "What is it time to do?" at any appropriate time. Obviously, you only ask him this question when you are actually going to take him to the potty and you are fairly certain that he will "potty" when he gets there. Also, you only ask him this question to refer to using the potty, and not to other events in the course of a day.

When your child can anticipate using the potty by answering your question, "What is it time to do?" you can move to the next step. Now you pretend to forget what it's time to do. For example, you get him up in the morning, remove his diapers, and then pause. In the past you have said, "What is it time to do?" Now you just pause. Perhaps he'll say, "Potty," or head for his potty chair. If he does, say, "Good, you can remember what it's time to do. You know it's time to potty." If he shows no signs of anticipating, say, "I can't remember. Is it time to get dressed? No . . . I can't remember. Is it time to make the bed? No . . . I can't remember. Is it time to brush your hair? No . . . ." Somewhere along here he may anticipate. If he does not, say, "What *is* it time to do?" This is a familiar question and he'll probably answer "Potty."

Continue trying to phase out your signal—"What is it time to do?"—by pausing, saying you can't remember, and asking other questions until your baby has taken almost full responsibility for anticipating this scheduled use of the potty. He will still have to learn to give you signals when he feels bowel or bladder pressure. The schedule training will likely have some correspondence with bowel and bladder pressure so that he will probably be getting some practice at reading these signals within himself already. The rest will have to be up to him.

SOCIALIZING

During the period from seven months to two years your baby will make phenomenal social changes. He will build up very strong ties with a few people while at the same time he may want to avoid strangers. He will begin to learn the social skills necessary to relate to a wide range of people— parents, grandparents, siblings, peers, shopkeepers, doctors, and friends. He will learn how to approach others and how to move away from others. His language skills will develop tremendously.

Socializing Play

As during his first six months, continue to make time in your schedule to play with your baby. Routine care time also provides opportunities for socializing play. Diapering, dressing, bathing, bedtime, and feeding are all times for games, talking, singing, and reciting. Other playtimes should also be a part of the day's schedule. Your job during this socializing play is to increase the amount of participation your baby shows. At first you'll do most of the initiating and maintaining of play interactions and he'll simply respond with coos and smiles. But soon he'll start imitating and participating in your socializing activities. Some early activities might include teaching him to cooperate in playing "Peek-a-boo" and "Patty-cake." Social greetings—"Bye-bye" and "Hi" are appropriate beginnings in social language. Teaching him to say "Mommy" and "Daddy" allows him to initiate a social interaction by getting someone's attention.

Teaching him how to get and hold someone's attention is an important social lesson. You are teaching him this every time you respond to him. If you often respond to him when he's fussing or crying and seldom respond to him when he's quiet or happily cooing or babbling, you'll effectively teach him that the way to get your attention is to be cranky and cross. On the other hand, if social attention is given when your baby is pleasant, you will find you have a baby who is often smiling, happy, and a pleasure to be with. He will have the beginning of the social skills that will enable him to initiate and maintain pleasant interactions.

STRANGERS

How do you expand these skills to others? The familiar people in his life will present few problems. As long as they are responsive, friendly, and moderately predictable to your baby, he will build up a social interaction with them also.

Very likely your baby will show fear and avoidance of unfamiliar people who try to approach him too close or too fast. He may cry or cling to you. He will make it very clear he wants nothing to do with "that stranger." If you're lucky, the "stranger" will be wise and hold off his approach. Then your baby will not be pushed to respond and will have time to get used to the unfamiliar person at a distance and be able to approach on his own time. If the "stranger" persists and your baby becomes more distressed, you'll have to advise the person to take it a little bit easier. You might say, "I think Carol would be happy to sit on your lap a little later. She needs time right now, though, to get used to you and feel comfortable about a new person."

The point is—when your baby, of whatever age, shows fear or avoidance of strangers, your job is to give him time to approach when he's ready and not force him into an interaction that is frightening to him. You will also have the job of encouraging him and helping him when he begins to show signs of being ready to approach a stranger. One thing you can do is tell the other person something to do to make himself less frightening. You could say, "I think Carol would walk to you if you'd hold that picture book open in your lap." Or you might suggest, "If you'd take Kevin to the kitchen to see your canary, he might be happy to have you hold him."

Encouraging your baby directly is a little more tricky. You have to be obviously present and available without focusing your baby's attention on you and away from the unfamiliar person he's trying to muster the courage to approach. It would probably not be helpful to say, "See, you can sit on Uncle Stan's lap and it is not even scary." But if you make it clear that you enjoy talking with and being with this person, your baby will sense your comfort. If you seem unconcerned about whether he clings to you or approaches the stranger, his curiosity will begin to get the better of him and he'll start to sneak a peek, then want down, and will probably eventually approach on his own. Once he does approach, he'll likely find that it can be fun. As he makes more attempts to approach strangers, he'll learn that most of them are friendly.

PLAYMATES

Your baby will probably show less hesitation in approaching unfamiliar children than unfamiliar adults. In fact, he may be quite eager to initiate play with his peers. Learning to play with peers is very important. Babies under a year seldom really interact with each other. They may enjoy being near each other and watching each other, but they seldom share activities. Truly cooperative play seldom occurs before age three. But your baby will still learn some social skills about peer interactions in playing near children who are approximately his age.

Your job in peer play is to provide suitable playmates (not too rough nor too easily pushed around) and then give your baby a chance to develop his own interactions. If you've taught him to initiate and maintain social attention by smiling and being pleasant, he'll be well on his way to getting along with his peers. There will undoubtedly be squabbles over toys, but these should be settled between the little ones unless someone is being hurt. Again, if you've taught your baby to find something else to do when one thing is denied, he'll handle those frustrations fairly well. And if your baby has not been taught that strong crying or aggression pays off when he's denied, he'll be unlikely to start a fight over a toy. So, what you teach him in his interactions with you will carry over to a peer relationship.

SEPARATION

As your baby becomes more social, he comes to value your presence. He clearly enjoys having you around. At some point he may show distress when you leave him. You may only be going out of the room for a moment or you may be leaving the house for several hours, but he cannot predict the length of your absence or anticipate your return. To him you are leaving and he wants you with him. You cannot, however, be with your baby constantly. He will need to be taught how to deal with separation from you.

There will be little separations every day—turning your attention from your baby to something else, moving at a distance from him, leaving his sight momentarily, and leaving him to fall asleep in his crib. If you handle these little separations well, you may never see any distress from your baby at times of longer separation. The general principle you want to teach is "Sometimes I will leave you and regardless of what you do, after some time I will return to you."

Taking that statement by parts, and starting at the end—"I will return to you"—is one way to clarify your job. Teaching your baby that you will return to him can be taught only through repeated instances of actually returning to him. He will not learn this in one or two trials. You will have to leave and then return again and again before he can begin to understand that you will always return. At some point, much beyond age two, you may begin to teach him that there is a slight possibility you may not return because accidents can happen, but this is not a target in the early years. In teaching your child to handle short separations, start by giving a signal that will affirm your intent to return. As you leave your baby, you can say, "I'll be right back," or, "I'll see you soon." This type of signal will be very helpful to your baby when he learns to rely on it.

The next part of the statement—"after some time"—is also taught with many instances. Sometimes your attention will be diverted for seconds, sometimes you will leave for moments, and other times you will be gone for hours or maybe even days. Before age two there is no way to explain to your baby just how long you will be separated from him. He will simply have to learn, through many instances, that sometimes it's a short time and sometimes it's a long time. If the separations are part of a repeating routine (for example, regular morning times with a baby-sitter), he will learn to predict the length of the separation and your eventual return. But there will be other times when the length of separation will be unpredictable. When you first begin to teach him to handle separation, you may find it helpful to plan for many little separations of short duration and then gradually lengthen the time. Your separations should eventually include a wide range of time intervals that are unpredictable. The requirements and routines of daily living will probably result in separations of unpredictable lengths without your doing much to make them so.

The first part of the statement—"Sometimes I will leave you and regardless of what you do"—can be the most stressful to teach. It may be difficult for you to accept the fact that you need not always be available to your baby at his bidding. You have every right to be unavailable sometimes. You may choose to be unavailable (to go shopping, for instance), or be forced into a separation (for example, hospitalization, attention to another family member). Whatever the case, *sometimes* you will be separated from your baby.

Helping your baby handle these separations is part of "regardless of what you do." If you have taught him early through many instances that you will return even after long and unpredictable absences, you may never see much distress at separation. He may always appear totally confident when you leave him. However, if distress does occur, your job is to let it be known that his distress does not undo you. You know you will return and the only way you can demonstrate that to your baby is to leave so that you can return. You will not reassure him by holding him, talking to him, and postponing the separation. If you get too involved in his distress, you are likely to increase its occurrence in the future by reinforcing it. So matter-of-factly, cheerfully, and confidently, assure him that you'll be back and then leave.

Part of your job for separations where your baby will be looked after by someone is to make sure that he will be properly cared for. This includes letting your baby get acquainted before you leave and giving complete enough instructions to his baby-sitter so that important routines are followed.

Through careful training, you can do much to avoid the strong emotional distress that can occur when you must leave your baby. It's your job to prepare him to handle such times.

SUMMING UP

During the time from age seven months to two years, you and your baby will have become a cooperative unit. You will be giving each other clear signals, reading each other's signals, and rewarding each other during daily interactions.

If you have done your job well, your baby will have become mobile and exploratory and you will have taught him appropriate limits to these activities. His frustration crying and his crying over little hurts will be at a minimum. He will be well on his way to being a good eater. He will seldom resist bedtime because you have taught him that bedtime is pleasant and resistance doesn't pay off. Toilet training may or may not be achieved but you will know how to do it when the time comes. You will have taught your baby to be cheerful and happy most of the time by not responding to fussing and crying for social attention. Your baby will have many skills for initiating and maintaining social interactions. When he is shy with strangers, you will know how to deal with this. Finally, you will be able to leave your baby with little or no distress on his part because you have taught him how to handle separation. In short, you have taught your baby to be a happy person.

9 | *How to Have A Smart Baby*

Teaching your baby the skills he needs to function in the world involves both the social skills covered in the previous chapters and the language and motor skills described in this chapter. Children learn what they are taught. They can be taught to be happy and they can be taught to be smart.

Babies do not inherit intelligence in the same way that they inherit curly hair or a small bone structure. They do inherit a nervous system, but what is learned is primarily dependent upon what is taught. Intelligence can be defined in terms of knowledge of language concepts, speech skills, and problem solving procedures. This knowledge is taught. A great deal of learning that constitutes intelligent behavior occurs before a child starts school. As a parent, you will have a tremendous influence on your child's acquisition of these skills.

Early teaching can pay off for your baby. He can learn that being taught is a rewarding, pleasant experience. He can take a "student" role very young and feel comfortable doing so. He can learn how to learn—how to pay attention, what to pay attention to, how to respond to questions and instructions, what to do when he makes mistakes, and how to receive correction and praise. "Little people" are often being instructed by "big people." If your baby can receive instruction well, he is in a position to be taught more. The more he is taught, the smarter he will be.

So your job in rearing a smart baby is teaching the skills that will allow your baby to function constructively and to teach those skills in a manner that will make learning pleasant so that he will readily approach new learning situations and thus increase his skills.

TRAINING ATTENTION

Your first task will be to develop your baby's attention. He needs to learn to focus his looking and listening. You start by just catching his attention for fleeting moments and then slowly building up the length of time he will attend to something. Paying attention is an extremely important skill. Many children who have difficulty succeeding in school have very poor attending skills.

THE NEWBORN

When your baby is a newborn, he will need practice in controlling his eye muscles to focus his visual attention. Placing objects in his range of vision will help develop this control. Toys and colorful objects attached to the side of his crib, level with his head, will provide an opportunity to focus his vision. Colorful, patterned bumper pads encourage visual attention. Placing your baby in different parts of the crib that face different directions will stimulate visual activity. Moving his crib to different locations now and then is also likely to stimulate visual activity.

Your newborn will also need some listening experience. For example, talking and singing to him, playing the radio, putting a clock near him, and leaving a musical toy playing in his crib will stimulate his listening. Too much constant noise is not desirable. You are trying to teach your baby to listen. If you bombard him with chatter and noise, he may learn to disregard what he hears as meaningless clutter. When he's no longer interested in *looking* at something, he can simply shift his gaze, and he will do this often in his early months. But if he's no longer interested in *listening* to something, it is not an easy task for him to divert his listening attention to something else. You need to help him sift out auditory signals and focus his listening attention.

AS HE GETS OLDER

As your baby gets older, you can expand the range of things you use to catch and maintain his attention. You can also expand the number of things competing for his attention at any one time. His changes in strength and coordination will do both of these things for his visual world without your doing much directly. As he learns to hold up his head, raise himself to his elbows and then to his hands in a prone position, roll over, and sit up, his changing positions will provide a wider, more competing range of things to look at. You can continue to do much to make his visual world detailed and interesting. His crib can be decorated, pictures can be hung on the walls, toys can be put in his hands, he can be moved from room to room, and he can have trips outside the house. All these things, and many others, provide a rich visual world.

Teaching listening also involves expanding the range of things to listen to and increasing the competing material. These things will also happen without your directly doing much about it as your baby is awake, alert, and social more of the time. As he becomes part of the family, he will also become part of a world filled with sounds—people talking, telephones ringing, door slamming, appliances roaring, clocks ticking, radios playing, dogs barking, wind blowing, water running, and traffic speeding by, to mention only a few. The range of volume and variety of sounds available to him in this noisy world will be vast.

ATTENDING TO PEOPLE

What he attends to in the range of visual and auditory material available to him is something you do not have too much control over. But you do have control over his paying attention to you and subsequently to other people. He must learn to listen to and look at you and others on request if he is to learn the other skills involved in intelligent behavior.

Teach your baby to look at your face by looking at his face. If you are in a face-to-face position, your baby will focus on your face for a few seconds. When he does, smile, shake your head a little, wiggle your nose, raise your eyebrows up and down, blink your eyes, or make a pleasant sound. His attention will be held by the changes that occur while he is looking at your face. Try to keep him looking at you for longer periods of time.

Teach your baby to listen to you by talking and singing to him. Talk to him quietly at first. Loud noises startle babies. Change inflection, rate, and volume to hold his attention. Usually we determine that we have someone's listening attention because he is looking at us. So you should teach your baby to look at you when you talk. Teaching looking and listening attention will go hand-in-hand for several months.

You should teach your baby to give you his attention when you say his name. This is easily done. You know some things that you can say, do, or show him that make him smile. So say his name, wait for him to look at you, and then reward his attention to you with one of your ways of making him smile. Maybe you simply say "Hi" in a very happy voice. Maybe you give him a big smile or jiggle your head. Maybe you show him a picture, a toy, or his bottle. Maybe you hold his hands and clap them together for him. Do different things at different times. Keep him guessing so he'll give you his attention when you say his name to see what you're going to do. Sometimes show him something immediately. Other times wait several seconds, holding his gaze, before rewarding him. This procedure makes more of a game out of your training and also leads to better attending.

After you have taught your child to attend when you say his name, you can begin to teach him to direct his attention where you want it. Say, "Earl," and when he looks at you, pause and then say, "Look," showing him an unfamiliar object or picture that you are touching with your finger. Later you can point to things very close to him but without touching the object, and then you can point to things increasingly farther to his right, left, in front, or behind him. You teach him first to attend to you, and then to direct his attention to some object. Focusing visual attention at your request is necessary before you can teach him to name objects or to otherwise talk about his environment.

You can also help your child direct his listening attention. Say, "Marty," and when he looks at you, say, "Listen," and then make an unfamiliar but pleasant sound—maybe a soft whistle, chuckle, click, hum. You can repeat this activity with many sounds and at many distances and directions from him. Attentive listening is essential for developing speech through imitation.

IMITATION

Teaching your baby to imitate actions and sounds is a very important job of yours. Many things your baby will learn will depend directly on his ability to imitate. Language skills in particular will develop out of imitation. Imitation training as described here involves four steps. When you first begin to teach imitation, you will be imitating your baby. That activity will lead directly into his imitating you after you imitate him. Then you'll be able to initiate a familiar gesture or sound and he'll imitate you. Finally, you will be able to initiate an unfamiliar gesture or sound and your baby will imitate you.

You Imitate Him

You can begin the first step—imitating your baby's gestures and sounds—as early in his life as you like. This is not to suggest that you imitate every sound and move he makes. Just imitate him a few times a day. When he rolls his head, you can roll yours; when he smiles, return the smile; when he gurgles or coos, try to imitate those sounds. When he begins to handle and manipulate objects, imitate his movements. If he puts a toy in his mouth, put a toy in your mouth; if he switches something from hand to hand, you do the same; if he bangs his toy or throws it, you imitate his action. He'll begin to notice your actions and may even look to see what you do *after* he does something. When you imitate him, let him know you think it is a game. Laugh and smile when you do what he does.

Repeating Exchanges

When he starts paying attention to your actions that follow his actions, you can begin the next step—engaging him in repeating exchanges of imitations. First you imitate him, then he repeats the action, then you repeat it, he repeats it, etc. These first repeating exchanges will probably be gestures rather than sounds. For example, try imitating your baby when he pats or slaps a table with his hands. First he pats, then you pat, then he pats again, etc. Don't be concerned about how many times or with what rhythm the

patting occurs. Just take turns patting. You'll probably suspect that he would have repeated patting the table whether
you had imitated him or not. That's probably true. But at
this very early stage of teaching imitation you have to start
where you can. Your goal at this stage is simply to build up a
repeating exchange where you take turns doing the same
thing. Some other activities that lend themselves well to this
goal are vigorous head nodding, clapping hands, waving bye-
bye, banging blocks together, bouncing in your chair,
squeezing squeaky toys, and throwing objects. You will be
able to discover others as you watch your baby.

When your baby has caught on to what game you're
playing when the two of you repeat a number of gestures,
you might be able to do the same thing with sounds. Of
course, before you can imitate him, he has to be making
some sounds spontaneously. His most frequent sound is the
one to concentrate on imitating first. It may be a repeating
consonant sound (b,b,b,b, or g,g,g,g,g,g), a sustained vowel
(aaaaa, oo-oo-oo--oo, ee-ee-ee), a nonvocal chord sound
(click, smack, sputter), or some other sound (oing-oing-oing
or bee-yub-bee-yub-bee-yub). Simply try to build a repeating
exchange when he initiates some frequent sound.

He Imitates You

If your baby will engage in a repeating exchange of some
activities he initiates, you will be ready to go to the next
step, even though he may not repeat any sounds with you.
Your next step is to get your baby to imitate you when *you*
initiate some *familiar* gesture or activity. At some point in
your playtime when you have *not* been playing your imitating game, say, "Kurt . . . look . . . do this," and do something
the two of you have taken turns repeating many times. If
he imitates you, say something that tells him you are
pleased and then repeat the gesture. Later try the same thing
with another gesture. If he does not imitate you, prompt

him by guiding his hands into the gesture. Keep trying, guiding him when necessary, until he will imitate a number of familiar gestures or activities that you initiate.

You should try to extend this step to sounds as well as gestures. If you have succeeded in the previous step with getting him to repeat turns saying some sounds that he initiates, you should have little difficulty extending those skills into getting him to imitate familiar sounds when you initiate. If you did not succeed in the previous step with sounds, but he does very well in repeating gestures and activities that you initiate, you might still try him at this step with sounds. Perhaps his earlier spontaneous babbling was not sufficient but is now adequate to build on. First, go back to the earlier step and see if you can engage him in a repeating exchange of sounds he initiates. He may learn this skill very quickly now. If so, proceed to the next step of getting him to imitate familiar sounds that you initiate. Say to him, "Bill . . . listen . . . say this," and then make some sound the two of you have taken turns repeating many times. Continue this training until he will imitate a number of familiar sounds.

If you have trouble getting your baby to succeed in either of the two previous steps with sounds, but you're doing fine with gestures, try this. Pair a gesture and a sound. Say, "Carl . . . look . . . do this," and make some familiar gesture *and* say some familiar sound. Maybe you vigorously nod your head and say "oo-oo-oo-oo." Maybe you clap your hands and say "mee-mee-mee-mee." At first your baby may simply disregard the sounds and imitate the gesture. Continue with the paired tasks, making your gestures more insignificant and your sounds more significant. Eventually your baby may imitate the entire pair. When he does, eliminate the gesture and simply request him to imitate the sound.

The procedure above may be helpful for babies who learn to imitate gestures before they learn to imitate sounds. If the pairing procedure does not work, simply keep trying to achieve the earlier steps in imitating sounds until your baby catches on. He will catch on, but maybe not as early with sounds as with gestures.

IMITATING "NEW" SOUNDS AND ACTIONS

The final step—teaching your baby to imitate *unfamiliar* gestures and sounds that you initiate—will take you directly into teaching your baby new skills. The routine is the same as for the previous step. You say, "Dale . . . look . . . do this," and then you make some gesture that the two of you have *not* repeated together. Choose something you know he can do but something he has not imitated on request. If he imitates you, say something to show that you are pleased. If he does not imitate, guide him into imitating you. Continue with this routine until he imitates new gestures and sounds when you introduce them.

All the four previous steps should be done in a way that is fun for your baby. You will get his best cooperation if the two of you have fun together. If you start very early, his training may cover a year's time. It is not something you are going to rush through at an early age. There will be times when there seems to be no progress in your imitation training. That may be entirely true. It may even be wise to stop imitation training for several weeks. Perhaps some very important and momentous changes are taking place in another area of your baby's life. Maybe he's just learning to take those first few steps alone. Maybe he's just learning to open things, and he's very busy opening cupboards, drawers, and boxes and exploring all the contents. Maybe he's "discovered" his big sister and he's following her everywhere.

TEACHING NEW SKILLS

When your baby can imitate sounds and gestures that he has never imitated before, you are ready to use this skill to teach him new ones. For example, you might start teaching him to name objects. The procedures for teaching this skill are described in a later section in this chapter, Teaching Language. You might also find it fun to teach your baby to say animal sounds. In addition to expanding his imitation skills, saying animal sounds teaches your baby to answer a complex question—"What does a cow say?" There is nothing about the word cow that directly signals your baby to say "Moo." He must "remember" after many repetitions that when you say, "What does the cow say?" he's supposed to say, "Moo." This is good language training for your baby. Also, he'll probably get lots of attention for this skill. Most people like to ask babies, "What does the_____say?" and hear their response.

Teaching routine for animal sounds. The routine for teaching imitation of animal sounds is this. Find out what animal sounds your baby can say fairly easily by asking him to imitate you. For example, say to him, "Mark . . . listen . . . say 'moo.' " Try several sounds—"peep-peep, baa, grr, bow-wow, moo, mew, oink," for instance. Choose one that he imitates fairly well and say, "Mark . . . listen . . . what does the *sheep* say? . . . say, 'baa'." Continue this routine for several days. Begin to make your pause longer and longer before you say, "Say, baa'," and see if your baby will anticipate and say the animal sound without your prompt. It may take weeks to teach the first one or two, but each additional one will be learned more quickly.

When your baby can answer the question, "What does the _____ say?" for his first animal sound without a prompt and has been doing it for several days, you can teach a second animal sound. Choose a sound your baby can say and one that is very different from the first one. The routine is the same as for the first animal sound. Your baby may show some confusion and, for instance, answer "Baa" for the cow and "Moo" for the sheep. Don't be alarmed and don't scold. Simply repeat the question and add your imitation prompt, "Say 'moo'," very quickly before your baby can make another error. Don't keep asking the questions over and over again. Your baby's certain to become confused or simply stop answering.

Adding additional animal sounds follows the same routine. Each new sound must be clearly differentiated from the earlier ones. When new sounds are added, your baby may seem to forget some of the old sounds. When he forgets or gets confused, simply repeat the question and give him the prompt.

Perfecting speech. A later use of your baby's imitation skills will be to help him perfect his pronunciation skills. Helping your baby speak clearly is something you need to handle very carefully. You will not enlist your baby's best cooperation if you are constantly correcting his pronunciation in a critical way. Your baby will try to speak clearly because the payoff for clear speaking is his being understood. So your job is to provide examples of clear speaking for him to imitate. (Baby talk obviously is not helpful to a baby trying to perfect his pronunciation.) When your baby says a word that is very difficult to understand, simply repeat the word *slowly* and clearly in the context of your baby's message. You can then ask a question that will require your baby to repeat the word. For example, your baby may say, "Me have ho-no." You know what he wants because you've heard him say this many times, so you say, "You want a *do-nut*. Okay. Here, what are you eating?" He may or may not improve his pronunciation after your demonstration. You simply continue to provide examples of clear speaking and give him an opportunity to try it.

MOTOR SKILLS

Part of being a competent individual involves the ability

to efficiently move around, explore, and manipulate things. The two previous chapters gave guidelines on how to provide a safe, nonfrustrating, encouraging environment for the development of mobility and exploration. This chapter provides additional suggestions.

GETTING AROUND

The mobility skills (rolling, crawling, creeping, walking, climbing, and running) develop in relation to the consequences provided by the physical environment. For example, one kind of rolling from tummy to back results in a head bang and another kind does not. For the beginning walker, certain postures and speeds result in many falls and other postures and speeds result in fewer falls. Your baby will learn to move around in the ways that produce the fewest hurts and the most successes. You will have to do almost no direct teaching of these skills.

So what is your job in developing your baby's mobility skills, in addition to providing a safe, nonfrustrating, encouraging environment? Your job is to *let him move*. You'll often be able to carry him somewhere faster than he could get there himself, but let him go on his own power as often as you can. When he's crawling and creeping, let him move from one room to another on his own. If you want him to change rooms, invite him to follow you. When he begins to walk while holding your finger, lead him where you want to go, don't carry him every time. When he's walking on his own, have him follow you or go with you as you hold his hand. If you need to go up or down stairs, let your baby navigate them too. If you are outside, let your baby walk on his own.

All these things will take more of your time. It won't always be possible or convenient to wait while your baby comes along at his own slow speed. You cannot let a beginning walker slowly cross a busy street holding your hand.

Sometimes your schedule will be tight and you cannot afford the time necessary for your toddler to follow you down the sidewalk to the grocery store. But when you can, allow time for your baby to move about on his own. The more he practices his motor skills, the more skillful he will become.

Another aspect of "let him move" is to allow your baby to keep trying new things even though you fear that he may fall, get bumped, or get stuck. He may not get into trouble, as you suspect, or if he does he may recover from a little hurt quite readily. This does not mean that you do not protect your baby from real dangers (open stairways, revolving doors, streets, children swinging, moving bicycles). It means that you do not block his movement to protect him from little hurts. If you can show him another way to go about something without blocking his activity, do so. For example, maybe you see your baby about to crawl headfirst off the couch. This could result in quite a bang. Quickly change your baby's position so that he's in a feet-first position and then help him scoot backwards until his feet touch the floor. You may have to do this many times over a period of several weeks.

Teaching your baby to walk is one task in which you can be of direct assistance. It will be helpful to him to spend time walking holding on to your fingers for balance and walking a short distance to you when he's ready to solo. At first, you will have to hold both hands and let him walk slowly in front of you. Then he will be able to balance holding only one hand at your side. Later he will walk alone while you are near. He may start toward you for two or three steps when you squat in front of him and hold out your hands to him. Your job is to provide assistance in balancing to whatever extent he needs it.

If you provide a safe, nonfrustrating, encouraging environment and let your baby move as much as possible—helping him when you can—coordination, strength, and endurance will improve as he moves around in his world.

EXPLORATION AND MANIPULATION

In addition to being able to move toward something, your baby will also need to learn to explore and manipulate things in his environment. These skills are primarily motor skills of the arms, hands, and fingers. They involve reaching toward, grasping, holding, and releasing objects, and various manipulative skills such as taking things out, putting things in, squeezing, pushing, pulling, poking, stacking, taking things apart, putting things together, buttoning, zipping, and scribbling.

Your job is to provide a variety of appropriate objects for your baby to explore and manipulate and to provide demonstrations, as they are needed, of how things work. As with mobility, many of the consequences for exploring and manipulating are built into the activities themselves. You will have to do very little direct teaching. For example, some ways of stacking blocks will result in a stable tower while other ways will result in a teetering tower that easily falls down. Your baby will learn to build stable towers by practicing with his blocks. You can provide appropriate blocks, give demonstrations of stacking blocks, and offer encouragement and support.

When your baby is only a few weeks old, he will start reaching toward objects. At first he will over-reach or under-reach and even when he gets his distance accurate he will only bat at the object. Soon he will begin to grasp things. As the months pass, his grasp will improve and he will be transferring objects from hand to hand and then releasing objects in a planned way. You can provide objects for him to practice his skills on.

A cradle gym across his crib will stimulate reaching, batting, and grasping. You can put things in his hands. He will drop things very quickly at first, but he will soon learn to hold things longer and in a position where he can see them. He will also put everything in his mouth, so give him things that are sanitary and large enough so that he won't swallow them or choke. Letting him help hold his bottle will be good training.

As his grasp improves, let him feed himself finger foods, such as crackers and teething cookies. At first you will have to put the food in his hand. He may drop it many times and not know what happened to it. Try to direct his attention to it, retrieve it for him, and put it back in his hand. Then later put the food near him and let him pick it up himself. Soon you will see that he begins to look for his cookie when he drops it and tries to retrieve it himself. When he has learned to reach for and grasp bits of food, try putting cereal pieces or cracker bits in a shallow cup and see if he will take them out. Later encourage him to take other small objects out of a container and then to put the objects into a container.

As part of your imitation training, encourage your baby to squeeze his squeaky toys, to push objects away from himself, and to pull objects toward himself. Use imitation to teach him to pull a string attached to an object out of reach to bring that object into reach.

One kind of manipulative problem solving that you can begin to teach your baby before he reaches one year is cause and effect, or "what I do has an impact." He will already have some notion of his ability to make an impact on his environment. He will probably be able to make noises happen by banging toys or make his cradle gym swing by batting at it with his hands. Help him expand this awareness. Show him how to release a jack-in-the-box. Help him pull the string on a talking toy. Demonstrate how to turn the water on and off in the tub and sink. Let him scribble on paper. Show him how to blow out a match or a candle. Show him how to push a light switch on and off as you hold him. Give him as many opportunities as you can to experience his own power in having an effect on his environment.

There are many, many manipulative toys available for babies less than two years old. Puzzles, form boards, form boxes, stacking toys, blocks, beads, dressing dolls, clay, pegboards, tool benches, and crayons are all appropriate. Every-day objects also provide manipulative experience. Some examples are pots, pans, lids, zippers, buttons, shoelaces, packages to open, drawers, doors, boxes with lids, books, water faucets, spoons, forks. You can demonstrate how these things work as your baby tries to successfully manipulate them.

TEACHING LANGUAGE

Teaching your child how to handle language—understanding what people say and making himself understood—is one of the most exciting tasks you'll encounter. This is not something you'll accomplish in a few months or a couple of years. You'll begin your instruction when your baby is a newborn and continue clarifying and building on the use of language all your child's growing years.

Talking to Your Baby

Talking to your newborn may seem ridiculous to you and something you only do in private. Maybe you really enjoy talking to your very little baby and feel that it is the right thing to do. In either case, imagine what would happen if you (and everyone else) refrained from talking to your baby until he was "ready to understand." Would he just suddenly attend to language and begin to make sense of these very new sounds in his environment that are being directed to him? Absolutely not. Understanding language signals is not an instantaneous acquisition.

So, what does the very young baby (less than six to eight months) learn when we talk to him? He learns that language is tied into almost every human activity, that it can be a pleasant, comforting set of sounds, and that the important people in his life use language to signal each other. It is necessary for him to learn these rather global things about language before he can focus on the parts of language, (words, phrases, sentences, questions, instructions) and learn to respond in very precise ways. His first responses to language will simply be to look at you when you talk and to appear relaxed and content. He will also be capable of responding in a distressed way if your voice is angry, loud, or harsh.

As you talk to your baby, he learns what language is and what it is for. He also learns that he can participate. When he starts cooing and babbling to you, you have the beginnings of a verbal interaction called a conversation. You teach him that when people talk to each other, first one talks while the other listens, then the roles are reversed and the first one listens while the other one talks. When your baby is "talking," don't interrupt. If he starts "talking" while you are talking, simply stop talking until he is quiet. You'll be surprised how quickly he will learn that in a conversation two people do not talk at the same time.

Touching Named Objects

Using language as signals to touch objects you name can probably be taught before your baby reaches his first birthday. Your baby's response will be to touch something when you say, "Where is the_____?" or "Show me the_____." Learning that things have names, that those names are the same no matter when and where we refer to them, and that when the name is said the thing is to be located and touched is a very complicated set of skills for your baby. Teaching the first few instances may take weeks or months, but each new instance will take less time to teach. Once your baby gets the idea, he will very quickly learn to touch new objects you name and will soon begin to ask, "What dat?"

Teaching your baby to identify a few body parts is the

easiest place to begin for several reasons. His body is always with him so you can sneak in little lessons anytime the two of you are together. You will not have to rely on special equipment or materials. Second, a great deal of care-taking is focused on his body—diapering, dressing, bathing, and feeding—so there will be lots of natural opportunities to teach names of body parts. Finally, body parts are easily pointed out to your baby. He can see most of them and he can *feel* you touch them.

The teaching routine goes like this. Choose a body part that your baby can see (hand, foot, tummy, knee, leg), touch that part, and say, "This is your tummy." Do it again: "This is your tummy." Then say, "Where is your tummy?" and guide his hand to touch his tummy. While he is touching his tummy, say, "You can find your tummy." (What you ask or say to get him to point or touch is your decision, of course. Whatever you say, it should always be the same. "Where is_____?" was chosen here because it seems to be a common form among people who talk to babies, and therefore it would be more likely that your baby would respond to other people's questions.) Repeat this routine often during the day, but not more than four or five times in a single "lesson." Pause before you guide his hand. He may touch his tummy by himself. Continue the routine until he will touch his tummy almost anytime you ask, "Where is your tummy?"

The second body part you teach should also be visible to your baby, but very far away from the first body part in order to reduce the possibility of confusion. If you teach *tummy* first, then *foot* might be a good second instance. If you teach *hand* first, then *arm* would not be a good second instance. The routine is the same. Touch your baby's foot, saying, "This is your foot." Do it again. Then ask, "Where is your foot?" and guide his hand to touch his foot. While he is touching his foot, say, "You can find your foot."

When you add a second body part to the teaching routine, you will very likely find that your baby makes mistakes.

He'll sometimes touch his tummy when you say, "Where is your foot?" and vice versa. When he makes a mistake, don't panic. Don't despair. Don't assume your baby is stupid or you're a bad teacher. This is a very hard lesson, though it must seem easy to you. So when he makes a mistake, calmly say, "I see you can find your tummy. Listen . . . Where is your *foot*?" Be ready to guide his hand if he makes no response or starts to point to his tummy again.

When your baby can touch two body parts on command with few errors, you can add a third body part. Again, the body part should be visible and at a distance from the other two. The routine is the same. Make sure the first three are well learned before going on to a fourth and so on. After four or five visible parts are learned, you can teach parts your baby cannot see (eye, ear, nose, mouth, hair, back).

When your baby has learned several body parts, you can begin to teach him to touch other objects when you ask, "Where is_____?" A second possible category of objects is food. Foods will be present only at mealtimes so "lessons" will be limited to a few times during the day. Another possible category is clothing. It is reasonable to be involved in teaching your baby items from both categories at the same time in his life but at different parts of the day. At mealtimes you may be asking about bananas, toast, meat, milk, or carrots, and during dressing and undressing you may be talking about shoes, socks, shirts, diapers, or pants. The routine is the same as for body parts. You touch an item of clothing and say, "This is your shoe." Then you ask, "Where is your shoe?" and guide his hand to touch the shoe. While he is touching the shoe, you say, "You can find your shoe!"—and show delight. The rules are the same. You teach one item until it is well learned before teaching the next. When you teach two items within a short period of time, you should teach objects as different from each other as possible. *Sock* should not be taught right after *shoe* and *toast* should not be taught right after *bread*. You confirm "right" answers. You accept mistakes calmly and correct them pleasantly.

After your baby can identify several body parts, food, and items of clothing with few errors, he has probably got the idea of identifying objects. He is now ready to identify pictures of objects in books. Again the routine is the same and the rules are the same. You will probably not have to guide his hand. He will know that when you ask, "Where is _____?" he is supposed to touch that thing.

POINTING TO OBJECTS

Pointing is another way of identifying objects. It is the response to use when the object is too far away to touch. Teaching your baby to point to objects is an easy extension of teaching him to touch objects to identify them. Identifying family members and pets may be the easiest category to start with. The routine is this. Point to (but do not touch) the person and say, "This is Daddy." Then say, "Where is Daddy?" Your baby may point. If so, you don't have to teach the response. If he does not point, guide his hand to a pointing gesture and while he is pointing say, "You can find Daddy." Repeat this routine until your baby can identify several people and pets by pointing when you say, "Where is_____?"

Teaching your baby to touch or point to things when you ask, "Where is_____?" gives you a routine to use to teach him to identify many objects in his environment and to know whether he understands you or not. If you simply said, "This is_____, this is_____, this is_____" about a number of things in his world and never taught him to make a response, you wouldn't know whether you were teaching him anything or not. Probably not, but you wouldn't know.

ACTION WORDS

Once your child can touch and point to objects, you can also begin to teach the actions we perform with objects such as, *"Bring* me the ball," *"Wave* to Grandpa," *"Kiss* the doll," *"Don't touch* that knife," *"Splash* the water," *"Knock* down the blocks." In teaching new action words, use objects you know he can identify so that there are not two tasks to learn at once. Start with an action you can easily demonstrate using imitation.

BLENDING SOUNDS

An interesting variation of the identifying objects routine and one that is useful in teaching your baby to listen attentively to parts of words is to present a "listen and blend" task. When your baby can identify a number of objects, people, and pets, say, "Where is your fff-oo-oo-oo-oo-t?" Say the target word very slowly, but keep the parts connected. If he doesn't respond, say it a little faster. Keep saying it faster until your baby gets it and touches his foot. Do this with many words until he can really listen and blend your sounds into words. "Listen and blend" can later be applied to other tasks besides identifying objects. This skill will be helpful to your child when he is being taught to read.

NAMING OBJECTS

Teaching your baby to name objects is your next big task. Your imitation training will be a great aid at this point, because part of the routine is already familiar to your baby. He will be ready to try to imitate you when you say, "Say _____." The basic routine for teaching your baby to name objects is this. Touch or point to the object and say, "This is _____. What is this? Say_____." When your baby imitates you, you say, "Good. This is _____."

This instruction will not always be as straightforward and simple as the routine above suggests. Sometimes your baby will not say anything when you say, "Say_____."

When that happens, do not insist or try to force him. Simply return to the earlier routine of asking him, "Where is _____?" and proceed to the next object you will ask him to name. After several days or weeks of trying to teach him to name objects, you will have found some few objects, among the many objects he can identify, that he will be able to name. Again, it's a problem of helping him get the idea. You must keep trying to teach him to name the objects he can identify until he learns what he's supposed to do. The first few instances will be the most difficult. It may take many weeks to teach your baby to name the first four or five objects. After that the rate will accelerate until he is learning to name objects, persons, and animals so quickly and from so many sources that you will be astounded.

NAMING ACTIONS

After your baby has learned to name objects and persons, you can begin teaching him to name actions. He has heard you use these action words for many months as you have described what you are doing with him and what he is doing —"*Peek*-a-boo," "*Sit* down here," "You are *running*," "Time to *eat*," "I'm *tying* your shoe," "*See* this picture," "Did you *bump* your head?" "Let's *ride* in the car," "Shall I *tickle* you?" These action words describe what people and things do. The routine for beginning teaching seems somewhat stilted because the customary question, "What are you doing?" calls for an "ing" type answer, (sitting, reading, running, etc.) and that is a bit too complicated for the first lesson. So you say, for example, "You eat. What do you do? Say 'eat'," or, "You read a book. What do you do? Say 'read'." When your baby can answer a number of such questions, you can teach him to use the "ing" form of the verb. Then you say, "You are eating. What are you doing? Say 'eating'." Soon you can begin asking him about the actions of other people, animals, and objects.

ADDITIONAL TEACHING STRATEGIES

The suggestions in this chapter are only beginning guidelines for rearing a smart baby. It is not possible to cover the necessary range of activities to be taught in a single chapter. Our goal is to introduce some ideas for you to follow up on. Two additional books are recommended. They are both filled with detailed descriptions of activities. The first book, *Teach Your Baby,* is written for the age range of newborn to thirty-six months. It includes activities for stimulating feeling, seeing, hearing, encouraging gross and fine motor development; teaching problem solving, imitation, self-awareness, speech, and language. The activities are clearly described and easily carried out at home. (*Teach Your Baby,* Genevieve Painter, New York: Simon and Schuster, 1971.)

The second book, *Give Your Child a Superior Mind,* is written for newborn through five years, with very little emphasis on the child before eighteen months. The activities in this book are more academic, or school-oriented. The preschool curriculum includes language training, reading, and arithmetic. (*Give Your Child A Superior Mind,* Siegfried and Therese Engelmann, New York: Simon and Schuster, 1966.)

SUMMING UP

The tasks described in this chapter are samples of some of the very important things you do with your baby from birth to about age two. Your baby is introduced to the skills he will need to function competently in his changing world. You begin by teaching your baby to focus his listening and looking attention. You teach him to pay attention to you and to other people and to direct his attention at your request. You simultaneously teach your baby to imitate. The four-step process to teach imitation covers many months.

You will see, however, that his imitation skills are very important as you begin to teach him to speak and to solve manipulative problems.

In teaching motor skills, you take primarily an encouraging role. You provide a safe, nonfrustrating environment to encourage your baby's developing mobility. You help him when you can to increase his mobility skills. You use patience and noninterference to allow him to move at his own speed and take his own small risks. In developing manipulation and exploration, you provide an abundance of objects for your baby. By demonstration and imitation you teach your baby to solve various manipulative problems.

Teaching language skills encompasses almost every activity of the day. Several routines were described in this chapter to teach specific tasks, such as identifying and naming objects and naming actions. In addition to these, your baby will begin imitating and using language for other functions. You teach your baby to use language by talking with him in ways that consistently and accurately represent the rules and functions of language.

Two additional books were recommended as sources of additional teaching suggestions. Both are full of detailed and tested procedures.

Teaching your baby intelligent behavior is a very rewarding and important task. The more skills your child has the more successfully he will function. At a bare minimum, he will need to handle language and to solve various problems. If you teach your child to be a successful learner who eagerly and confidently approaches new learning situations, you will have done something extremely important for him and his future.

10 | *Toward Self-control*

With progress in language development, it becomes reasonable to start teaching children to guide their own behavior according to probable consequences. Children can be taught to make choices wisely and to plan ahead. The first step is to teach rules for behavior and the reasons behind them. Rules specify the conditions under which certain behavior should or should not occur and the social consequences for following or not following the rule. Reasons specify the existing relationships between behavior and consequences (social as well as natural consequences). The rule might be, "If you are ready for bed by eight o'clock, I'll read you a story." A social reason for getting ready for bed then would be to hear a story. Natural reasons for getting ready for bed would be to get some rest and not be so tired.

After children learn something about rules and reasons for behavior, intelligent management of one's own behavior becomes more likely. The next steps are to set up protected opportunities for choice-making and planning, and finally to permit the child to manage some consequences on his own.

TEACHING ABOUT REASONS

If you teach about reasons first, you can later use the reasons to help reinforce the learning of rules. In teaching about reasons, you want to teach your child to verbalize the relationship between behavior and consequences. This can be done in three phases:

1. Start by verbalizing for the child the relationship between behavior and consequences as examples occur. (The reader should note that this is the same as using behavior-specific praise and punishment, as discussed before.)

Examples involving social consequences:

- "You got ready for bed on time, so you get to hear a story."
- "You ate all your dinner, so you can have some ice cream."
- "I'm giving you ten points for making your bed."
- "You hit Mary, so you will have to go to your room for five minutes."
- "You got dressed all by yourself. I'm proud of you."

Examples involving natural consequences:

- "You didn't watch where you were going, so you fell down and got hurt."
- "You did not eat your dinner when it was offered. That's why you feel hungry now."
- "You stayed out in the sun too long. That's why your skin burns."
- "You took a good nap, so now you feel all rested and strong again."

2. The next step is to ask your child to give the reasons he was rewarded or punished.

- "Why am I reading you this story?"
- "Why am I sending you to your room?"
- "Tell me why you are hungry now?"
- "What made your skin all red like that?"

Reinforce correct answers to questions by repeating the whole statement, "Yes, I'm reading you a story because you got ready for bed on time."

3. When your child can give reasons about specifics, tie these into more general rules. Relate a series of specific examples to more general rules where appropriate. These general rules can include most moral precepts.

- "Yes, I'm reading you a story because you got ready for bed. When you do things that please me, I want to do things to please you."
- "Yes, I am punishing you because you hit Mary. I can't allow you to hurt other people."
- "Yes, you get ten points because you made your bed. When you work hard and do your part, you get rewarded."
- "Timmy let you borrow his bike because you let him play with your truck. When you share with people, they often want to share with you."
- "Yes, you burned your fingers because you touched the stove. Stoves are hot. Hot things can hurt you."

TEACHING RULES

Many implicit rules are present in what parents decide to reinforce and punish in the early years. By the age of three for most children, it should be possible to begin to make rules for daily living more explicit through verbal instruction. There are several advantages to this. When the rules are explicit, it is easier for parents to be consistent in their use of rewards and punishments. When the rules are explicit, it is easier for children to learn what is expected of them. The rules help to summarize a lot of specific behaviors in a few words. Training for living involves learning to give, to share, to do one's part, to follow instructions, to keep clean, to eat right, to dress according to the weather. Rules can simplify this very complex task by providing guidelines.

The rules you will need to codify will usually involve social consequences. Natural consequences will usually take care of themselves, except in the case of dangers that could seriously harm or kill a child. It is a good idea to give your child a role from the start in setting up the rules that you currently are working on. Hold a family meeting to discuss new training goals with your child. Express your view that you think it is time for Jimmy to be doing more things on his own since he is growing up. Suggest one or two rules that you would like him to work on for the next few weeks and discuss possible consequences. Give your child a voice in the decisions. As rules are mastered, shift the rules to new problem areas. A weekly family meeting provides a good basis for revising the focus of concern from time to time and allows input from all family members. It also begins the process of teaching cooperative negotiations.

How to Make Rules

The first key to making rules is to keep in mind the parts of the basic learning episode: SIGNAL $\longrightarrow$ BEHAVIOR $\longrightarrow$ CONSEQUENCE. But instead of talking about a specific signal, we will treat it more generally as the set of conditions, or situation, in which behavior is to occur. The rule should specify:

A situation → *A behavior* (set of behaviors) → And *a consequence*

- Weekday mornings (situation), get dressed and ready for school (behavior) before coming to breakfast (consequence).

It is implied that the child would have to go back and complete the task before eating should he come to breakfast not dressed for school.

- Before each meal, wash your hands and face before coming to eat.

- After each meal, brush your teeth to earn two points.
- When put to bed, getting out of bed, will be fined five points.
- In play with other children, hitting will be punished by a five-minute time–out.
- After school, homework must be completed before going out to play.
- After dinner, dishes must be washed, before watching TV.

The next key to making rules is to state them in such a way that it is easy to tell if they have been followed. This means you have to get specific about just what you mean by "doing dishes," "cleaning your room," or "dressed and ready for school." If you do not spell out the specifics, you lay the basis for arguments of the "Yes-I-did," "No-you-didn't" sort. Clear rules insure that a half-completed job will not be reinforced, thus teaching bad habits.

- Each morning, make your bed to earn ten points. By "make your bed" I mean top sheet folded back over the blanket, sheets and blanket tucked in neatly and smoothly, and pillow in place.
- On Saturday, clean the recreation room before having friends in to play Ping–Pong. Cleaning involves putting away all toys and games, straightening out the furniture, dusting the tables and window ledges, and vacuuming the floor.
- If you play cooperatively with Billy this afternoon, you can watch TV for an extra thirty minutes tonight. Being cooperative involves sharing your toys, taking turns, and not fighting or arguing.

How to Use Rules

The keys to the effective use of rules are to start them one or two at a time, to provide lots of reminders at the beginning, and to ignore protests. When a child breaks a rule, ask him to tell you the rule he broke and require that the correct behavior be completed if that is possible.

Many of the procedures described in Chapter Four for the use of token systems automatically insure the effective use of rules. Statements of how to earn points and lose points can both specify the required behaviors and serve as reminders. Charts of progress also serve as reminders to both parents and children. In fact, it is strongly recommended that parents who are already into many problems with their children about rules and responsibilities actually start to rectify the situation with a formal token system because it gives more reminders to both parents and children. Reminders are prompts, and good teaching requires that prompts be faded when they are no longer needed. In this case, the formal token system with charts and fixed rules can be slowly shifted to a weekly allowance based on maintenance of responsible behavior. The charts and points are faded out, but the rules for responsible behavior continue to be enforced on an informal basis.

Some parents will object to the statement "ignore protests." We don't mean you should ignore your child, but just be careful about not reinforcing argumentative behavior. As long as the rules are reasonable, even though they involve a change for your child, stick to your guns in a matter-of-fact way. "That's the rule. I've got all day if you have, but we're going to do it." Children learn to get to parents with charges of "unfairness" because feelings of guilt lead parents to respond to such charges with attention and counter argument. Avoid the trap.

When a rule is broken, either the rule has not been learned or the consequences have not been effective. The correction procedures for broken rules should first assume the rule has not been learned. Have the child repeat the rule he has broken. Tell him the rule and have him repeat it if he cannot do it on his own.

• Timmy jumps in bed and asks to hear a story before

putting away his toys. Mother asks, "What's the rule, Timmy?"

"Put away my toys before the story," says Timmy.

"That's right. Why don't you do that?"

Timmy jumps out of bed and puts his trucks and cars in the toy box.

After the broken rule is repeated, require completion of the correct behavior when possible. If completion of the correct behavior is not possible, require some form of restitution. A child can be required to go back and brush his teeth or comb his hair. The forgotten chores can be completed. At the dinner table, failure to ask politely can simply lead to noncompliance with the request until a polite request is made. If the rule is concerned with messing, damaging, or hurting, restitution should be considered. A mess can be cleaned up, a damaged article can be paid for, and an apology can help undo a hurt.

ANTICIPATING TROUBLE

Once a child is able to talk about rules for behavior, it becomes possible to prepare a child for better self-control in a difficult situation by discussing beforehand what is expected of him. For example, in the past when you've gone to an amusement park, the kids have gotten so excited and have begged and pleaded for "more rides" or "more Coke" to the point of irritation. It is possible to reduce this kind of struggle by discussing the rules beforehand and getting promises and agreements. "We will each have seven rides to choose. When your tickets are gone, there will be no more rides. And each of you has fifty cents to spend on other things. When that's gone, don't ask me for money for an ice cream cone. Are the rules understood? If you can follow the rules, we will want to take you out more often."

The key to anticipating trouble is to think ahead to what is coming that might lead to trouble and then discussing rules for conduct in the quietness of home rather than in an involved or exciting situation. Common trouble situations are trips to stores, parties with guests, other children visiting, going to the doctor or dentist, staying with a sitter, visiting friends, and long trips in a car. After preparing your child for trouble situations and subsequent good behavior on his part, be sure that you let him know how pleased you are with his grown-up behavior.

GIVING CHOICES

Having progressed in the learning about rules and reasons, your child is also ready to begin making more choices on his own. In making a choice, a child must decide which of two or more courses of action to take by evaluating the probable consequences of each action. In the example given above, the children had to decide which rides to take and how to spend fifty cents. The problem that arises is that you can't do or have everything. If you choose A, you can't have B. If you choose B, you can't have A. So it is important to choose wisely.

The choices open to children should be gradually increased as competency and responsibility progress. Initially, parents make all decisions in all areas. Eventually children are completely on their own. Consider first the area of clothing. At first mother decides everything. Then the child might choose what to wear for some occasions, but mother decides about important occasions and does all the buying. Eventually, the child may be allowed to buy his own clothing. Similar progressions are found concerning foods to be eaten, friends to associate with, sleep habits, work-study responsibilities, and use of free time. The important point to be made is that parents need to plan for this gradual increase in self-responsibility for decisions. Children need to gradually be allowed to make their own choices and learn from the consequences of those choices. In thinking about current objectives for your child, keep in mind the question, "What new choices can I allow him to make this month?" At some point, when your growing child asks you, "Do I have to do my homework now?" you will want to be able to answer, "That's up to you. You know the consequences, so you decide."

SELF-MANAGEMENT OF CONSEQUENCES

Experimental study of self-management has not yet progressed far enough to give sure guidelines concerning effective training procedures. Some studies have shown that children can be trained to record their own behavior in school and administer tokens to themselves according to an appropriate rule. In general, however, children initially are not accurate evaluators of their own behavior (they tend to underestimate their misbehavior) without training. One would also guess that children would provide for themselves larger rewards than parents would if they were not trained to do otherwise. As in any other area of behavior, it is necessary to train children to evaluate their own behavior objectively and to manage consumption of reinforcers wisely. Training toward this end can be accomplished at home by gradually giving the children a larger voice in evaluating how well they have met their responsibilities and what consequences would be appropriate.

Some of this training can be accomplished within the context of a token system. At some point, the consequences for appropriate behavior could be simply money that the adolescent would have to manage to cover clothes purchases, transportation, school lunches, dates, and other needs. The amount required would be negotiated periodically to give planning experience. Failure to manage wisely would have very direct and meaningful consequences that could increase wisdom in the future. Training in self-evaluation could be accomplished by having an older child record responsibilities he has met. This would initially be verified by parents to train accurate recording. Later the accuracy would be checked only occasionally.

While some training in self-management of consequences can be provided through the use of a token system at home, we seriously doubt that this can do the whole job. There is still need for careful training in evaluating comparative values. What is more important to long-term happiness:

Honesty or money?
Sexual excitement or trust?
Power or friends?
Love or success?

The church has traditionally attempted to provide training in this area, but in our opinion such training has not been very effective. In some ways, scouting has been more effective for some children. For the most part, however, the task still falls on parents. The teaching of rules and reasons is a step in the right direction. Providing good models of value priorities is another. What is needed additionally is experience in living with peers, where give and take is necessary and mutual support is essential. Various camps and well-supervised group programs can help in this area.

In any case, as a parent, be forewarned that value training is a key ingredient in effective self-management, and you will need to include such training in the educational plan for your child.

SUMMING UP

As language develops, it can be used to help learn better

self-control. Begin by teaching your child about the reasons for behavior. Verbalize the relationships between behavior and consequences; ask your child to tell you about the reasons certain things happened to him; and then tie these reasons into more general rules or moral precepts.

The next major step, once a beginning understanding of reasons exists, is to begin the teaching of rules of conduct. This can start with a few very simple requirements for self-care or a contribution to household chores. Eventually the training should encompass all important aspects of social living. Make your child a part of the training through the use of a family meeting to set up goals and consequences.

In making rules, specify a situation, a behavior, and a consequence; be sure the behavior is so specified that you can be sure the rule has been followed or not.

In using rules, start them one or two at a time, provide lots of reminders at the beginning, and ignore protests. When a rule is broken, ask your child to tell you the rule he broke and require that the correct behavior be performed.

Self-control can be further enhanced by discussing beforehand with your child what to do in difficult situations. Alternatives are considered and commitments made to avoid conflicts. Another step to take is to provide increasing opportunities for choices in which the child must take full responsibility for the consequences of his choices.

Finally, steps should be taken to insure training in accurate self-evaluation of behavior and in management of consequences. One way this can be provided is through the use of a token system at home.

Beyond these steps, parents need to provide young adults with experience in living with peers, where give and take is necessary and the values and conflicts associated with closeness to others can be experienced.

11 | *Problems in Social Interactions*

As children grow and learn, they often develop patterns of interacting with others that adults consider to be problems. In this chapter, we examine a number of such problems to further show how the basic principles of behavior can be used to analyze and correct such problems.

DEPENDENT BEHAVIOR

Johnny is a four-year-old who was brought to a clinic after his nursery school teachers reported that he was aggressive when the teachers or children were not attentive to him.[1] At home, his mother reported that he was not aggressive. In fact, he usually stayed close to mother most of the day. Johnny asked lots of questions and asked mother for help on many tasks. Mother was very responsive to Johnny and kept a close watch on him. She often interrupted his play to see that he was all right. Mother said she was afraid Johnny might get into trouble with his playmates or break things in

161

the house, so she kept a close watch. She preferred to have Johnny at her side.

His teachers believed that Johnny became aggressive when he didn't know what to do, and he seemed to need others to tell him what to do. Also, his teachers and other children were probably accidentally reinforcing his aggressive behavior by the attention they provided to it. This all suggested that Johnny's mother was keeping him overly dependent upon her for answers to little problems, such as what to do next. In other words, his mother was reinforcing an interaction that was keeping Johnny too protected.

At the clinic, the nature of the problem was explained to Johnny's mother. She was taught to give praise and attention to independent behavior and respond less to dependent behavior. Independent behavior involved playing alone and doing things without asking mother for help. A measure of Johnny's dependent behavior showed a rapid decline as mother learned to reinforce independent behavior. Johnny never showed aggressive behavior during these clinic sessions.

Parents do most things for very young babies. They have to if infants are to survive. However, when parents continue to help children with tasks they could be taught to do themselves, parents are in effect encouraging their children to remain babies. To avoid this problem, encourage your child to *try* to help himself from the start. An important goal for parents in the early development of their child should be teaching self-help skills as the child is physically capable of learning them. Other goals should focus on learning to play by oneself, choosing alternative activities, and learning to give and take with peers.

Note that the problem of dependency is usually twofold. First, there is likely to be parent reinforcement of a dependent form of behavior, and second, there is likely to be the child's skill deficiency in independent behavior. Often it is necessary to both withdraw attention from dependent behavior and teach new skills related to independence.

Examples of reinforcing dependent behavior:
- Johnny and his mother as illustrated above.
- Billy and Jane were less than a year apart. Anytime Jane wanted something, Billy would read the cues and ask on her behalf. As a result Jane would just point and say "Ooog" everytime she wanted something, and she got what she wanted with Billy's help. To correct this, it was necessary for their parents not to respond to Billy's words but to insist that Jane tell them what she wanted before giving it to her. At times it was necessary to prompt her so that she was helped to say the words.
- Nearly every day after school, Chuck would ask his mother to "Help me with my homework. I don't understand it." This would usually save Chuck from reading the instructions, and he could get through faster with mother's help. After awhile mother found that he could do it by himself, and she refused to help. Chuck got very upset and could not do his homework. Mother stuck to her guns and simply said that he would have to stay in until he figured it out himself. When he finally finished, she looked over his work and praised Chuck for doing his homework by himself.

Examples of overcoming skill deficiencies:
- If we want children to get dressed or undressed by themselves, we need to take time to teach them how to work buttons and zippers.
- If we want children to feed themselves, we have to teach them how to use knives and forks and spoons.
- If we want children to play cooperatively, we have to teach them to take turns and follow the rules.

The next three case studies illustrate variations on the theme of dependent behavior problems. They are especially interesting because of the procedures used to change the problems.

CLINGY POLLY

Polly was a three-year-old in a special nursery school.[2] Although physically well developed, her behavior was unusual. She would participate very little in the preschool program. She would not play with other children, use the names of other children, nor touch them. She rarely used outdoor play equipment. With teachers, she would usually hang onto a coattail and speak a type of baby talk that was an imitation of her younger brother's speech. Polly's parents were not native speakers of English, and this may have helped to prevent Polly's use of English with peers. After three months in school, no improvement was noticed, so a special program to help her was started.

It was decided to try to increase Polly's use of outdoor play equipment. This was selected as a key behavior because it was likely to increase opportunities for interaction with other children. At first the teachers would bodily place Polly on a piece of play equipment and hold her there for thirty seconds, giving appropriate social reinforcement and staying near her. A different piece of equipment was used each day. Polly got lots of attention as long as she was using some play equipment. This "priming" was dropped after a week or so, and social reinforcement only was used to keep play going. Gradually, teacher attention was made more intermittent (to help teach Polly to play more on her own). Over the two months of the study, Polly's time using the play equipment when outdoors increased from zero to an average of 70 percent. But what was important were the related changes in interactions with peers. Touching other children, talking to them, and cooperative play all increased substantially. Baby talk and other baby behaviors decreased to near zero.

The strategy of reinforcing a key behavior that increased the likelihood of more peer interactions was very effective.

Furthermore, it could be expected that Polly's changed behavior would continue because of the new reinforcers provided by peers.

Another interesting aspect of this study centered on more traditional interpretations of Polly's behavior. Her baby talk and other imitations of baby brother would likely be interpreted by some as regressive behaviors—signs of emotional disturbance requiring psychotherapy. The simpler explanation is to view her baby talk as an imitation of her brother's behavior. When adult attention to such behavior was removed, the baby talk disappeared.

When a new child arrives, many changes occur for the older child. As noted with Polly, a model of less mature behavior is provided and might be imitated. This might include wanting a bottle again. Often the older child is provided with less attention and support, which can be upsetting. Such upset is usually called jealousy. There are several steps that can be taken to prevent jealous reactions. First, prepare the older child for the fact that mother will be gone for awhile. Second, while she is gone, father should give special attention to the older child and help to maintain contact with mother by phone. Third, when the baby is brought home, be sure the older child gets enough attention. Give the older child responsibilities for helping with the care of the new baby. Fourth, if babyish behavior appears, don't make a big deal out of it. If your child wants a bottle, let him try it. He'll soon find it is a pretty slow way to get milk. If other baby behavior occurs, treat it as nothing exceptional or unusual.

School-phobic Karl

Karl was afraid to go to school or stay there unless one of his parents stayed with him.[3] At seven, he had attended first grade for only a few days. He had had similar trouble attending nursery school. He would only play in the immediate vicinity of his home, frequently checking to see if mother was still there. Attempts to use "bribes" and threats had failed to keep him in school. Essentially, Karl got very upset when separated from his mother, and his struggles to have her stay with him usually were reinforced. Consequently, he learned to make stronger and stronger protests when separated from her.

Karl was taken to a clinic for help. The essence of the treatment was to reinforce "leaving mother," "being a big boy," and "going to school." This was accomplished at first by using doll play to set up imaginary situations in which Karl could be encouraged to have more "big boy" reactions.

At his first session in the clinic, Karl would not go into the playroom without mother. His teeth chattered, and he clenched one fist while holding mother tightly with his other hand. The therapist set up a "pretend" situation in which a doll named Henry was used. The therapist would ask Karl how Henry felt and what he was going to do. If Karl replied that Henry was not afraid and he would stay with the doctor, Karl earned a piece of candy as a reward. Other themes involved having Henry leave mother and walk to school and also to stay home while mother went shopping. Mother remained in the doorway of the playroom. At the end of the session, mother was advised to praise Karl for staying in the playroom and to work on praising Karl for staying outdoors more than thirty minutes without checking on mother.

By the end of the second session, Karl announced that his parents could stay in the reception room next time. Father reported that Karl had stayed outdoors playing for a whole hour. The parents were advised to continue to reinforce independent behavior and to borrow some first-grade books and encourage Karl's interest in them.

In the next seven sessions, the therapist worked with Karl on fears of being hurt by other kids and led him in "pretend" situations involving going farther from home. A visiting teacher was contacted to help Karl with beginning reading skills. The following slightly edited excerpt from the tenth session helps give a better picture of what the doll–play sessions were like.

E: What shall we have Henry do today?

K: Well, we could have him go to school.

E: Yeah, I think that's a good idea to have some work on going to school again today. That probably is the hardest thing for him to do. O.K., here he is (picking up the Henry doll). Where is Mamma? Oh, here she is (sets up blocks and furniture). Ah, maybe we had better have little Henry start off from home. When he does go to school, we won't have him go into the classroom today; he'll just run errands for the principal; no reading or writing this time. So little Henry is talking to his mother and he says, "Mom, I think I'll go to the school for a little while today." What does Mom say?

K: O.K.

E: Is he afraid when he is right there talking to Mamma?

K: No. (One candy reward.)

E: And so he gets on his bike and says bye-bye to Mamma. He stops halfway to school. What does he think now that Mamma is not there?

K: Ma-amma (laughs).

E: Yeah, but what does he do? Does he go back or go on to school?

K: Goes to school. (One candy.)

E: Yeah, that's right, he goes to school. Little Henry would go back and look, but big Henry would go on to school . . . and he goes to the principal's office and says, "Hi, Mr. Principal. I thought I would come back to school for a little while. Can I run some errands for you . . . ?" Henry gives a note to a teacher; then he comes back to the principal's office. He stops. What is he thinking about now?

K: Mamma is not there again.

E: Yeah, he is scaring himself again. Now, does he go back to the principal's office or does he go home?

K: He goes back to the office. (One candy.)

E: Yeah, that is right, he does. At least big Henry would do that; little Henry would get scareder and more scareder; but big Henry feels pretty good. "I am back, Mr. Principal." The principal says, "Why don't you go down to the cafeteria and get a glass of milk? I don't have any more errands for you to run right now." So he goes and is sitting here drinking his milk. What does he think about now? Every time he is alone he thinks about this.

K: Mamma again.

E: That's right, he always thinks about Mamma. Does he go home?

K: No. (One candy.)

E: That's right, he doesn't. Big Henry doesn't go home.

K: (Laughs) He sure is big. . . .
   A few moments later:

E: . . . and he is lying there on the sleeping mat. What is he thinking about?

K: Mamma. No, I don't think so because he got a nice neighbor [child] next to him.

E: So, he is not thinking about Mamma.

K: Nope. (E was too surprised to get reinforcement in on time.) About five minutes later:

E: Well, Karl, what have you been doing at home like big Henry?

K: Well, ah, yesterday I done some numbers (very excited) and I went up to a hundred. (One candy.)

E: You did! Good (with emphasis). What else did you do like big Henry?

K: I made a cake . . .

E: Were you outside playing yesterday? Of course it was stormy yesterday.

K: Yes, I was outside playing.

E: Did you think about Mamma when you were outside?

K: Uh-uh. I wasn't thinking about Mamma. (One candy.) I'm not thinking about her now either. (One candy.)

In the past few sessions, several play sequences had been devoted to little Henry's return to school for an hour or so with his visiting teacher. The possibility of Karl's actually doing this had also been discussed with him.

Between sessions eleven and twenty-three, Karl made his first trip to school with his special teacher. Then she gradually left him in the room by himself for longer periods. Support for his "big boy" behavior and bravery was given by parents and therapist alike. After a week, he told his parents he would not be afraid to go to school by himself and stay one hour, and he did. Later he announced he would stay in school all day by the end of the week, and he was able to. The clinic visits were terminated shortly after this. A follow-up three months later showed no fearfulness and a great improvement in his general adjustment.

With professional help in staging the steps of a transition from clingy, frightened behavior to school attendance, Karl made a dramatic change in a short time. The principles used to help Karl were basically those being taught in this book—a step-by-step reinforcement of behaviors approaching going to school and leaving mother. The only new procedure involved was the use of reinforcement of responses to *imaginary* situations to help prepare Karl for taking steps toward independence in real life.

THE BATTLE OF ROBERT AND SUSAN

In the following case study, Robert teases Susan, Susan runs to mother, and mother reacts to Susan.[4] Susan was reinforcing Robert's teasing with her strong reactions, and mother reinforced Susan's reactions by attention to them. An eventual solution was found when mother decided that Susan had to solve the problem of Robert on her own.

Before dinner each evening, Robert, who was twelve, had begun to tease sister Susan, who was ten. Robert's behavior was subtle. At times he would stand next to Susan, staring at her, until she reacted. At other times he would get a book he knew Susan was reading and declare, "I had it first." Sometimes he would just be in Susan's way and take a little too much time moving.

Susan's reactions were intense. She would scream and yell at Robert and protest to mother. Mother in turn would tell them both to stop it, but it did not stop. Robert would say, "I'm not doing anything," and mother was stuck with nothing specific to stop. Robert even told mother that he probably would not do it if Susan did not react so much. After a few days of this, Susan was constantly running to mother with complaints.

At this time, mother was taking a course in behavior principles, and she began to realize how she was maintaining Susan's behavior, which kept Robert going. She decided that the solution was to ignore Susan's complaining. She told Susan, "I'm sorry, it's your problem. You'll have to solve it yourself."

For the next three days, Susan kept coming to mother to complain. As mother ignored the complaints, Susan began to get more upset and yell at mother. Mother simply replied, "It's your problem." Susan was most intense on the third day. On the fourth day she gave up more quickly, and on the fifth day she was overly polite, trying a new tactic to get mother to punish Robert.

On the sixth day, Susan tried once to get mother's attention to her problem and then accused mother of "not loving" her. She threatened to run away. Susan left the house while the others had dinner. An older sister told mother Susan was in the yard.

After dinner, mother joined Susan under a tree in the yard to have a talk. Susan was feeling sorry for herself. An outcome of the discussion was a suggestion from mother that Susan completely ignore Robert's teasing. Susan tried this the next day. Now it was Robert's turn to get "the treatment." Robert became more obvious in his teasing, as subtle teasing did not work. Susan would just get up and walk away, saying nothing. Mother praised Susan for her new efforts. The next evening, Robert quit teasing after Susan ignored him a few times. A little later they were playing a game together at Susan's invitation. Mother told them how pleased she was to see them cooperating with each other.

In the next six weeks, only two little incidents occurred. Susan handled both of them without running to mother.

AGGRESSIVE BEHAVIOR

Many different kinds of behavior fall under the label of aggression. In previous chapters we have given examples in which aggressive behavior such as bossing and fighting have been changed through a change in parental use of reinforcement and punishment. Our goal at this point is to review more specifically some ways of preventing or eliminating behaviors of concern to parents.

Most aggressive behavior occurs because it works. In the face of an obstacle that blocks reaching a goal, an emotional reaction occurs intensifying behavior. If a more intense reaction overcomes the obstacle, it is more likely to be used in the future. The obstacle may be physical, like a stuck door, or social, like a parent saying "No cookie." The "more intense reactions" that occur in the face of obstacles are likely to be labelled "aggressive." Imitation of the behavior of others often determines just what is tried in a given situation. There are four classes of reactions: negative, tantrums, bossing, and fighting.

NEGATIVE REACTIONS

Negative reactions are common in the two-year-old who is constantly getting into trouble and being blocked by parental "Don'ts." The child reacts to these blockings of his actions with anger and protest. Very often parents will give in to the protests, thus reinforcing them.

Negative reactions can be reduced or prevented in two ways. First, by focusing on positive guidance of your child, anticipating trouble situations, and suggesting alternative activities before your child gets into trouble, you eliminate the need to frustrate your child with "No" and "Don't." Thus negativism can be reduced by reducing the occasions on which it can occur. Second, negative reactions can be reduced by being consistent about "Don'ts" when you must use them. If you mean "Don't," back it up and do not reinforce the protest behavior if it occurs.

TANTRUMS

Tantrums are intensified negative reactions. They become intensified through a series of learnings in which reinforcement is denied, protest occurs, and the parent gives in only after the protest is made more strongly. That is, parents inadvertently reinforce stronger and more violent protest reactions. Consider this example. Tommy wants to go out and play in the yard. Mother doesn't want to go out and supervise him. Tommy tries to open the door and go out, and she stops him. He gets angry and tries to get away. When this fails, he falls to the floor and cries. Mother feels sorry for Tommy, picks him up, gives him a hug to show that she loves him, and decides to take him outside. The next day Tommy wants to go outside, and mother says "No." Tommy gets angry and flops on the floor and yells. Mother doesn't like this, so she lets it go on for awhile. Tommy yells more and kicks more. Again feeling sorry and guilty, mother gives in, comforts Tommy, and takes him outside. Repeat this episode a few more times in a few more situations and Tommy will have learned to control mother through the use of tantrums.

Tantrums can be prevented in the same way that negative reactions usually are prevented by reducing provocation and withdrawing reinforcement for such reactions. To eliminate tantrums, you should use a time–out procedure. Properly followed, a time–out procedure can eliminate tantrums in three or four days. Tell your child that if he has a tantrum he will have to stay in his room until he is quiet and ready to join the family. Be sure the room is free of dangers and desirable toys. When a tantrum starts, simply say, "You will have to stay in your room until you are quiet." Take him there physically and shut the door. If he comes out before the tantrum has subsided, take him back and shut the door. Keep attentive and try to watch what is happening through the keyhole or by careful listening. Be prepared for a loud show the first day or two. When tantrums have paid off for some time, it may take thirty to sixty minutes for the first one to subside. The next one should be half as long, and they should become quite short after the third or fourth one fails to pay off.

Extinguishing tantrums requires a persistent parent, but the reward to the parent is worth the effort. A common outcome is a much more positive parent-child interaction, especially when reinforcers are used to encourage desired behaviors.

BOSSING

Bossing is a form of aversive control. When parents boss children, they give an order and if it is not obeyed, they back it up with a stronger punitive reaction until compliance is achieved. Children learn to boss from the models set by their parents and because parents often let their children boss them. The child who has learned to control his parents through tantrums is also likely to find that his parents obey a bossy order such as "Take me outside" before the tantrum occurs.

Taking a positive approach is one step in the right direction of preventing bossiness. Not accepting bossy orders from your children is another. When your child uses a command statement, suggest a request that might achieve the same goal and require that the request be used before honoring it. At the dinner table, mother doesn't respond to "Gimme," but does respond to "Please pass the . . ."

FIGHTING

Hitting, pushing, and biting are common responses designed to get others out of your way when you are blocked from doing something. Such responses are often strengthened by adults, as when a father wants his boy to be strong and tough, or if such behavior is necessary to survive when interacting with peers. In games and war, hand combat skills are often highly praised. While not wrong in itself, fighting is not acceptable in most social settings. As with other forms of aggression, the key to reducing or preventing its occurrence lies in presenting good models and controlling the consequences for fighting behavior. That is, reinforce cooperative behavior, do not let the fighting pay off, and if you must punish fighting, do so by withdrawing reinforcers rather than hitting your child.

SUMMING UP

The prevention and elimination of problems in social interactions provide further illustrations of use of the principles central to this book. The key to understanding dependent behavior problems is the recognition of the role of reinforcement for immature behavior and the likelihood of skill deficiencies. Most often adult attention and unneeded help maintain dependent behavior. The examples of clingy Polly, frightened Karl, and the battle of Robert and Susan were used to show variations in dependency problems and their solutions. The focus of problem solutions is on the reinforcement of more grown-up behavior.

Four classes of common aggressive problems were examined. Negative reactions and their blown-up counterpart, tantrums, can be avoided by parents being more positive themselves in the first place, and by being consistent in not reinforcing protests. Once tantrums become entrenched, a punishment program may be required to get rid of them. Bossy behavior is usually learned by modeling a bossy parent. Often too, bossing is maintained because parents find it easier at the moment to comply with their child's bossing than to ignore it. The cure lies in reinforcing polite requests in lieu of commands when your child needs your help. Fighting is controlled by following the general suggestions for the use of punishment to weaken a behavior. That is, reinforce compatible behavior such as cooperation, do not let fighting pay off, and if you must punish, do so by withdrawing reinforcers.

12 | *Special Concerns of Working Parents*

This chapter looks at the requirements for providing good care for your children when both parents work or must otherwise leave their children in the care of others. How can you insure adequate care of your children and maintain a strong relationship with them, when at the same time you must, or choose to, leave their care partly to others? The basic problems to be faced are: (1) providing for substitute caretaking appropriate to each child's current development; and (2) maintaining a strong, affectionate parent-child relationship.

PROVIDING ADEQUATE CARE

Locating adequate care for the children of working parents is a top priority activity. Different kinds of child care are appropriate for meeting the needs of children at different ages. A very young child needs more consistent individualized care so that child and caretaker can learn to read each other's signals. An older child needs more opportunity for social and physical activities. Some families with children

176

widely dispersed in age will have to decide what makes the most sense in their case. It may involve using more than one kind of care or it may be that one kind of care does a fairly good job of meeting everyone's needs.

THE INFANT AND PRESCHOOL CHILD

The three most important aspects of care for infants and preschoolers are an abundance of attention and stimulation, unhurried physical care, and a continuous and stable relationship with adults. Given these requirements, what is needed is a relatively permanent baby-sitter who is not caring for a large number of other children. The alternatives are a baby-sitter who comes to your home or one to whom you take your child. In either case, you will need to choose someone with whom you can cooperate in childrearing. You will probably want to choose someone who has similar styles and values in parenting. Determining the personal characteristics of a sitter can be done through references, interviewing, observing the sitter handling children, or all three.

Choosing the baby-sitter is an important activity. Aside from practical and convenience considerations (cost, location, transportation, promptness, flexibility of schedule), you'll want to know that she can establish a good relationship with your children. It would be desirable to set up a trial baby-sitting period, during which time you could stay home and inconspicuously observe the manner in which the sitter carries out her duties.

Once you've chosen a sitter, the next task is to begin the working relationship that allows you to continually train her in the way you want your children handled. In the case of an infant, you want her to be able to read your baby's signals, to teach your baby new signals, to play with and stimulate your infant, and to provide good physical care. You will want to show her how to handle feeding, bathing, diapering, bedtime, and playtime. You'll need to teach her what to do when your baby cries. In short, you'll be teaching the sitter to handle your infant in ways that are consistent with your methods.

If your children are a little older, you will need to teach a sitter who comes to your house your daily routines, the rules of the house, and methods of discipline you use. If you use a sitter outside your own home, you will mainly need to teach her about your children, not about routines and rules. She will have a schedule and set of rules for her own home. It will be her responsibility to accommodate your children to her household. This can be done more easily if she knows what your children prefer to play with, when they're accustomed to sleeping, what they like to eat, and what special routines they enjoy and count on.

Dealing with the concerns of infants and preschoolers about your absence can be quite matter-of-fact. If you are secure and satisfied with their care while you're gone, you can demonstrate this to them by making the good-byes warm but not dramatic. Occasionally there may be some distress at your leaving, but it need not become a serious problem. Chapter Seven discusses how to deal with separation from small children.

The Nursery School Age Child

When your child reaches the age of three or four, a new option is often available in the form of a nursery school or daycare center. Group settings such as these often have the advantages of having personnel trained in child care, nursing services, play equipment appropriate for development of physical skills, opportunities for learning social skills, and a somewhat structured daily routine designed to give variety and balance.

In choosing a nursery school or daycare center, take the time to visit and observe the program. Ask about the training background of the staff and the goals of the program as the director sees them. Explore the kitchen and food service, rest areas, and play areas. Are the facilities adequate for good weather and bad weather? What are the special rules about sickness? What health services are provided? Is a prior examination by a physician required? Is there enough staff? (There should be at least one adult for each five to eight children.) If you are lucky enough to have a choice, take the time to shop around. Your decision is important.

A baby-sitter may still be your choice for the nursery school age child because of cost, the presence of a younger child in the home, or because that is the only option available. If a sitter is your choice, give careful consideration to the availability of other preschoolers for your child to play with and to protected outside play areas for the development of large muscle skills.

Whatever your decision, keep in mind your responsibility to inform your temporary caretakers of what they need to know about your children's special needs, routines, and the unusual daily happenings important to understanding your child's behavior. Also take time to find out from your caretakers whether your children are happy, what problems are encountered, and what new behavior is occurring that you might want to support at home, or at least talk about with your children. Work together with them to solve any problems that may arise and to make the experience as enjoyable and growth producing as possible for your children.

Be sure to take time to talk to your children about any new arrangement coming into their lives. Prepare them for new situations by stressing the fun activities they can provide and the opportunities to do new things with new friends. And *continue* to talk with your child about his experiences in his new setting.

THE SCHOOL AGE CHILD

Child care for school-age children usually involves after school help until one or both parents return home from work. Two types of help are commonplace. One involves having a sitter at home to stay with the children and the other involves having the children go elsewhere until the parents are home. The children could go to a neighbor, a sitter, a relative, or a daycare center. They could attend some after-school function or some combination of the preceding. Their needs are primarily the following: (1) having some guidance and supervision appropriate to their age and independence level, and (2) having someone familiar to count on if they need assistance or permission.

Whatever type of help is appropriate for your family situation, your main responsibility will shift from teaching the sitter how to manage the children to teaching the children how to manage themselves with the help of a supervising adult. The children will be more independent and capable of moving about the neighborhood and community. They will have wider interests and school friends. They should have responsibilities. (Some details on teaching children to be responsible for themselves were provided in Chapter Ten.) It is possible to teach self-management and self-control without your being present all the time. You need only to assign the new responsibilities, provide an appropriate incentive, and have a way to check to see if they are carried out. You will want to teach your older children to let others know where they are, to behave with concern for others and their own safety when on their own, to keep track of their belongings, to come home on time, to do their chores, and so forth. To be a good teacher, you do not necessarily have to be there all of the time, but you do have to know what is going on.

THE HARD-TO-MANAGE CHILD

Children with handicaps, chronic illness, or unusual behavior problems may be difficult to handle in the usual child–

care settings. If you are faced with a difficult-to-manage child, be sure to check public resources available for the professional care of the difficult child. There are federal, state, and local government programs that may meet your needs at low cost. To learn about such possibilities see your pediatrician, your community clinic, a department of special education in a nearby university, and your coordinator for United Fund agencies.

MAINTAINING A CLOSE RELATIONSHIP

The nature of the relationship between parents and children is primarily a function of the quality of the interactions and the parents' positions of influence and responsibility, not the amount of time spent together. Working parents have the same opportunity to establish and maintain a strong, affectionate, influential relationship with their children as do nonworking parents. However, because of fatigue, tight scheduling, and outside obligations, a special effort may need to be made to keep the parent-child relationship positive and functional.

There are several ways that the parent-child relationship can be kept strong. One thing that parents can do is to insure that they hold the primary responsibility for making decisions about the children and to let that responsibility be clear to the children. A second means of assuring a strong relationship is to provide physical and emotional care (reinforcers) and to share important events, ideas, and interests. Establishing family "traditions" for both everyday events and special events helps maintain the relationship through having fun together.

PARENTAL RESPONSIBILITY

Dozens of decisions are made every day for and about

your children. The person who makes these decisions will have an impact on who is important to your children. To keep yourself in a position of importance, you need to keep responsibility for most decisions and not turn this responsibility over to someone else. This does not mean that parents must make all decisions about their children and that caretakers should make none. The children should know, in fact, that in their parents' absence, the caretaker is in charge of them. But the children can be made aware that the parents hold prime responsibility by having the caretakers consult you frequently in the children's presence. Also, if the children hear you tell the sitter what the routines are, how discipline is handled, what the menu is, and what the activities for the day are, they will know that you hold primary responsibility. It will be clear that even in your absence you have concern for what happens to them. Your sitter can also make it a practice to defer answers to some questions or decisions until the parents are available. For example, she might say, "We'll have to check that with your mother tonight."

For older children, it makes sense to include them in the decision–making process as much as possible. The family unit can share the responsibility. You might even want the children to help describe the routines and activities to the sitter. Again, you will be making clear to the children that the primary responsibility for decisions and planning rest within the family.

Another thing you can do to make your responsibility clear is to maintain the duties and functions of parents. This includes such things as taking your children to the doctor and dentist; visiting school on open house day; signing report cards; attending performances, plays, and recitals; dispensing allowances; taking your children shopping for school clothes; and attending mother-daughter and father-son banquets. If your children know they can count on you for the important functions that parents provide, you will have an important ingredient for a strong and influential parent-child relationship.

CARING AND SHARING

The glue that holds people together is mutual reinforcement—providing social, physical, and material reinforcers to each other. The parents who take a positive approach with their children will find that in the process they have built a strong relationship. Caring and sharing are descriptive of two important components of a strong positive relationship. Caring involves many of the behaviors discussed earlier under the topic of how to be a good reinforcer. Sharing involves taking the time to do things together. For the working parent, it may take some special effort to create the times for showing caring and for sharing.

A key to showing you care is to take the time to really listen to your children and take their concerns seriously. Listening and communicating may take only a few seconds or minutes, but you need to be open to it when your children want to talk to you. An understanding smile, a comforting pat, a clear restatement of their message, or a hug may communicate your caring and let your children know that you're with them. Children have joys and sorrows. If they know that you can understand their feelings, they come to understand their own feelings better and they feel very close to you as you help them understand themselves. Both Haim Ginott[1] and Thomas Gordon[2] describe in detail how parents can improve their communication of caring to their children.

It is also important for parents and children to share enjoyable times. This may involve good conversation at dinnertime, playing games, vacationing, planning and carrying out a project, singing around the piano, preparing meals together, shopping, hiking, entertaining friends, or any other activities in which members of the family enjoy what they're doing. In a family where both parents work, it may be necessary to carefully set aside time for the family to spend together. One way to help make this happen is to establish family traditions.

Establishing family traditions are just special ways of doing things at special times and places. These traditions might happen each day or on special days. Some examples of everyday traditions might be breakfast together, sharing of the day's plans, packing lunches together, looking over homework, feeding the animals together, dinner together, recreation after dinner, a familiar bedtime routine, or story-time. Special day traditions might include Sunday breakfast out, Wednesday church night, Saturday outdoor activity, Tuesday the kids cook dinner, every third week visit Grandma and Grandpa, have friends in for Thanksgiving, eat turkey sandwiches for breakfast after Thanksgiving, or give unbirthday presents on anyone's birthday. The idea is for you to consider establishing traditions your family counts on to be part of their lives and provide special opportunities for sharing.

SUMMING UP

Two major responsibilities of working parents are providing adequate substitute care for their children in their absence and maintaining a strong, affectionate relationship with their children.

Adequate care for infants and toddlers involves individualized attention and stimulation, loving physical care, and a stable relationship with a minimum number of caretakers. Older preschool–age children can profit from social interaction with peers as long as the adults remain attentive and involved. School-age children need someone to guard their safety, provide appropriate supervision and assistance, and grant permission when necessary. Parents must choose care for their children according to what best meets their needs.

With infants and young children, the parents need to work closely with the baby-sitter or other caretaker to assure that the children are receiving adequate, consistent care. For older children, the focus shifts to working closely with your children to teach them to manage themselves in cooperation with a supervising adult.

Maintaining a strong, positive parent-child relationship involves keeping the responsibility for family and child-related decisions, providing physical and emotional care, sharing important events and interests, and establishing some family traditions to provide continuity and times for sharing.

13 | *Changing Problem Behavior*

In this final chapter, we examine some of the steps to follow to achieve a behavioral change. We begin with a discussion among Doug, Linda, and a psychologist named Jane, who has been helping them work out a plan to teach Jimmy to behave better.

Doug and Linda were so pleased with their progress with Jimmy that they wanted to know if there were ways the same ideas could be used to make their marriage better. Jane agreed to help them try.

Doug got right down to business. "Look Jane, we want to know how we can learn to be more positive with each other."

"We're not unhappy with each other," Linda said, "but it seems to both of us that we could do a better job of supporting each other."

"I think that's just great," said Jane.

"Well, what do we do?" Doug asked.

"You could start by finding out what is going on," said Jane. "If you could get a daily record of behavior, you could see where you are and whether or not you are improving. The record would give you a basis for reinforcing each other."

"How do you record stuff like what we do with each other?" Doug wondered.

"You could just put marks on a card in your pocket," answered Jane. "Then you might need to summarize them each day on a chart or graph."

"You mean, make a graph like we do with business trends?"

"Exactly, Doug," said Jane. "The vertical axis represents the number of behaviors per unit time and the horizontal axis is used for successive days."

"Hand me that pad, and I'll show you what I mean." Jane then proceeded to sketch this graph:

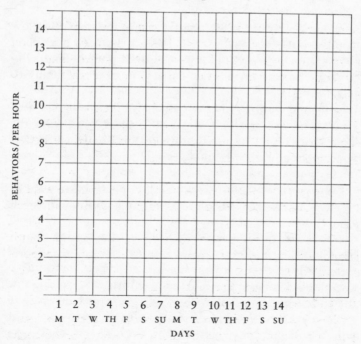

Jane continued, "Let's say you decide to count how often you say something positive to each other. You need to record the time period during which the counting occurs, say 6:30 to 9:30 in the evening, and the number of behaviors that occurred, say ten. Behaviors per hour would be ten divided by three hours, or 3.3. That would go on the graph like this." Jane put in the point for Monday. "You can make the scale fit whatever you are counting."

"I understand that part," said Doug. "What's the next step?"

"You have to get very specific about what you want from each other." Jane answered.

"I know what I want," said Linda. "I want Doug to show more appreciation for the things I do for us."

"Okay, Linda, exactly what do you do that Doug should appreciate more?" Jane asked.

"I put a lot of effort into cooking, which Doug neglects to mention. Another thing I do that Doug doesn't seem to appreciate is keeping our home pleasingly decorated. And when I shop, I do a lot of comparative shopping to try to save money. He seldom knows about this. But most of all, I don't think he shows enough appreciation for the fact that I have three jobs—wife, mother, and business woman. Even though my mother keeps Jimmy during the day, these are still a lot of jobs for me, and I think Doug should show more understanding and appreciation by helping me more."

"Now wait a minute," Doug said, trying to get a word in.

"Hold it, Doug. We'll get your side in a minute. That was good Linda—you said you wanted Doug to pay more attention to what you do in cooking and to let you know what he likes about it. You want him to notice more of the special things you do to make your home pretty. You want him to know more about your shopping efforts and to support them, and you want him to give you credit for your work in three jobs. Now you've gotten down to some specifics that will help Doug know better what he can do to make you happier. There's a further step in getting specific, but let's hear Doug's side."

"She makes it sound like I never say anything nice to her, and that just isn't so," said Doug.

"We know that, Doug," answered Jane. "Right now I asked Linda to be specific in pinpointing the things she does that should please you but for which she is not getting reinforced. Now I want you to do the same thing."

"Okay, I see what you're doing."

"Doug, are there areas where Linda could do more to reinforce you?" asked Jane.

"I don't need praise the way Linda does," Doug answered. "I know if my work is going well or not. . . . Jimmy reinforces me when I spend time with him, so I don't need praise for that. I just can't think of any specifics. . . ."

"You're always telling me you think we should make love more often," said Linda.

Doug looked embarrassed. "You don't mind if we talk about that with Jane here?"

"No, Doug," Linda said.

"Well, ever since Jimmy came it's hard to find time for each other when one or both of us is not exhausted or sick. I would like Linda to plan her week to give exclusive time to me during part of the weekend and a couple of times during the week."

"Good, Doug," said Jane. "Those are some specifics you can work with. Now suppose the two of you make an agreement—a contract—I'll change this way, if you'll change that way and take data for two weeks to see what the progress is like."

"A contract might read like this," Jane went on. "During the next two weeks, I, Linda, promise to create five occasions during which I will devote my exclusive attention to my husband, etc. . . . and I, Doug, promise to remark about at least one thing that pleases me during dinner each evening and to put Jimmy to bed on alternate evenings. The exact details have to be in agreements you make, but that's the idea."

"That has potential," said Doug. "I noticed that your example didn't try to do everything at once. You seemed to pick out some easily reached goals to start with."

"You were listening," Jane said.

"That kind of an agreement would really motivate me," said Linda, "because it's important to me to keep my promises."

"I like the fact that it's reciprocal," Doug noted. "It's fair, in that each of us is working to learn to please the other more. I write contracts every day, but I never thought about using the idea to make a marriage better."

"The contract helps provide clear reminders about what you are working on, and it sets up reciprocal reinforcers to motivate you to change," Jane explained. "You may still need to practice new behavior . . . like paying attention to what Linda cooks and using descriptive praise effectively. In other words, I don't expect miracles the first time out, but work on improvements."

"I think it will be sort of fun to work out a contract with you, Doug," Linda said with a smile.

Doug replied in a jokingly stern voice, "I drive a hard bargain!"

Jane got them back to the subject. "Okay, now that you have specified some behaviors to change you'll have to re-think the recording process. You won't need counters to deal with the kinds of behaviors you have specified . . . making love, putting Jimmy to bed on alternate evenings, and at least one compliment on cooking each evening."

"Could we just mark a calendar?" Doug asked.

"That's a good idea," Jane said. "You are dealing with yes-no events. They happen or they don't. So checkmarks are all you need to keep score. Counters and graphs are useful when you are more concerned about how often something happens every hour or every day."

"Well, we might try that later," said Linda, "when we work on rate of positive comments, but I would rather start with this simpler procedure."

"We could up the rate of lovemaking," Doug said with a grin. "That should give us practice in the use of counters and graphs."

"It looks like I'd better be leaving," said Jane.

"Gee, Jane, we do appreciate your help. I'm eager to try out these new ideas," Linda said.

"I'll check with you soon on your progress," Jane said. "Good night."

Through this story we have attempted to illustrate the basic components of a strategy for changing behavior. The key steps are these:

1. *Specify* the behavior to be increased or decreased. Do it in a way that you can be sure the behavior occurs or not.

2. *Record* how often the behavior occurs before a change is made. How many times a minute, a day, a week, does the behavior occur? Graph the frequency data.

3. *Provide consequences* for a change. Use any of the many kinds of procedures detailed in this book. Don't forget that token systems and contracts can be used to mutually reinforce changes between husband and wife or between parents and children. Be sure to specify carefully what consequences will follow what behaviors.

4. *Evaluate* the effectiveness of your change procedure. Continue to record rate data to show whether there is progress or not.

5. *Try again* if your recording shows the first procedure is not working. Maybe you can be smarter next time and find a procedure that will work better.

BE A GOOD PARENT: TEACH YOUR CHILDREN

References

Chapter 2   Consequences Count

1. Wahler, R. G.; Winkel, G. H.; Peterson, R. F.; and Morrison, D.C. Mothers as Behavior Therapists for Their Own Children. *Behavior Research and Therapy*, 1965, 3, pp. 113–124.
2. Zeilberger, Jane; Sampen, Sue E.; and Sloane, Howard N., Jr. Modification of a Child's Problem Behaviors in the Home with the Mother as Therapist. *Journal of Applied Behavior Analysis*, 1968, 1, pp. 47–53.
3. Homme, Lloyd E. Contingency Management. *Educational Technology Monographs*, 1969, 2, (No. 2) p. 4.

Chapter 3   Principles for Using Reinforcers

1. Hall, R. Vance; Axelrod, Saul; Tyler, Lucille; Grief, Ellen; Jones, Fowler C.; and Robertson, Roberta. Modification of Behavior Problems in the Home with a Parent as Observer and Experimenter. *Journal of Applied Behavior Analysis*, 1972, 5, pp. 53–64.
2. Ibid.
3. Adapted from Christophersen, E. R.; Arnold, Caroline M.; Hill, Diane W.; and Quilitch, H. R. The Home Point System: Token Reinforcement Procedures for Application by Parents of Children with Behavior Problems. *Journal of Applied Behavior Analysis*, 1972, 5, p. 487.
4. Ibid. pp. 485–497.
5. Wolf, M. M.; Giles, D. K.; and Hall, R. V. Experiments with Token Reinforcement in a Remedial Classroom. *Behavior Research and Therapy*, 1968, p. 6.

6. O'Leary, K. D. and Becker, W. C. Behavior Modification of an Adjustment Class: A Token Reinforcement Program. *Exceptional Children*, 1967, p. 33.

CHAPTER 4   ON BECOMING A REINFORCING PARENT

1. Becker, W. C.; Madsen, C. H., Jr.; Arnold, Carole R.; and Thomas, D. R. The Contingent Use of Teacher Attention and Praise in Reducing Classroom Behavior Problems. *Journal of Special Education*, 1967, 1, pp. 287–307.
2. Madsen, C. H., Jr.; Becker, W. C.; Thomas, D. R.; Koser, Linda; and Plager, Elaine. An Analysis of the Reinforcing Function of "Sit Down" Commands. In *Reading in Educational Psychology* (R. K. Barker, ed.). Boston: Allyn & Bacon, 1968.
3. Thomas, D. R.; Becker, W. C.; and Armstrong, M. Production and Elimination of Disruptive Classroom Behavior by Systematically Varying Teacher's Behavior. *Journal of Applied Behavior Analysis*, 1968, 1, pp. 35–45.
4. Becker, W. C.; Engelmann, S.; and Thomas, D. R. *Teaching: A Course in Applied Psychology*. Palo Alto, Calif.: Science Research Associates, 1971.
5. Ginott, Haim G. *Between Parent and Child*. New York: Avon Books, 1969.

CHAPTER 5   PRINCIPLES FOR USING PUNISHMENT

1. Thorne, G. L.; Tharp, R. G.; and Wetzel, R. J. Behavior Modification Techniques: New Tools for Probation Officers. *Federal Probation*, 1967, 31, pp. 21–27.
2. Christophersen, E. R.; Arnold, C. M.; Hill, D. W.; and Quilitch, H. R. The Home Point System: Token Reinforcement Procedures for Application by Parents of Children with Behavior Problems. *Journal of Applied Analysis*, 1972, 5, pp. 485–497.
3. Wahler, R. G. Oppositional Children: A Quest for Parental Reinforcement Control. *Journal of Applied Behavior Analysis*, 1969, 2, pp. 159–170.
4. Thorne, G. L.; Tharp, R. G.; and Wetzel, R. J. Behavior Modification Techniques: New Tools for Probation Officers. *Federal Probation*, 1967, 31, pp. 21–27.

CHAPTER 11   PROBLEMS IN SOCIAL INTERACTIONS

1. Wahler, R. G.; Winkel, G.; Peterson, R. F.; and Morrison, D. C. Mothers as Behavior Therapists for Their Own Children. *Behavior Research and Therapy,* 1965, 3, pp. 113–124.
2. Buell, J.; Stoddard, P.; Harris, F. R.; and Baer, D. M. Collateral Social Development Accompanying Reinforcement of Outdoor Play in a Preschool Child. *Journal of Applied Behavior Analysis,* 1968, 1, pp. 167–173.
3. Patterson, G. R. A Learning Theory Approach to the Treatment of the School Phobic Child. In *Case Studies in Behavior Modification* (L. P. Ullmann and L. Krasner, eds.). New York: Holt, Rinehart & Winston, 1965.
4. Kirk, D. Unpublished paper, University of Washington, 1965.

CHAPTER 12   SPECIAL CONCERNS OF WORKING PARENTS

1. Ginott, Haim G. *Between Parent and Child.* New York: Avon Books, 1969.
2. Gordon, Thomas. *Parent Effectiveness Training.* New York: Peter H. Wyden, Inc., 1972.

Annotated References for Parents

Becker, Wesley, C. *Parents are Teachers: A Child Management Program*. Champaign, Ill.: Research Press, 1971. 144 pp.; Bibliography.

This is a programmed text for parents. It may be used as a self-teaching device for those who wish to master the principles presented in this book. Order from Research Press, P.O. Box 3327, Country Fair Station, Champaign, Illinois 61820. ($3.75, discounts on orders larger than four. *Parents Are Teachers—Group Leader's Guide* available at $2, discounts on orders larger than four.)

Patterson, G. R.; and Gullion, M. E. *Living with Children: New Methods for Parents and Teachers*. Champaign, Illinois: Research Press, 1968.

A short programmed book to teach basic behavioral principles to parents. Order from Research Press, P.O. Box 3177, Country Fair Station, Champaign, Illinois 61820. ($2.50 plus postage.)

Tharp, R. G.; and Wetzel, R. J. *Behavior Modification in the Natural Environment*. New York: Academic Press, 1969.

A presentation of behavior modification principles as applied to troubled children. Many practical suggestions are provided through examples. Order from Academic Press, 111 Fifth Avenue, New York, New York 10003 ($10.)

Whaley, Donald L.; and Malott, Richard W. *Elementary Principles of Behavior*. New York: Appleton-Century-Crofts, 1971.

An excellent book that covers basic behavioral principles. Whaley and Malott motivate the reader with the use of much good humor. This is used as a college text by many. Order from Appleton-Century-Crofts, Educational Division, Meredith Corporation, 440 Park Avenue South, New York, New York 10016 ($7.45.)

ACKNOWLEDGMENTS

Hall, Axelrod, Tyler, Grief, Jones, and Robertson. Table 1, Page 24; Figure 1, Page 26; Figure 2, Page 29. From Modification of Behavior Problems in the Home with a Parent as Observer and Experimenter, *Journal of Applied Behavior Analysis*. Used by permission of the publisher.

Christophersen, E. R.; Arnold, C. M.; Hill, D. W.: and Quilitch, H. R. Table 2, Page 32; Figure 1, Page 62; Figure 2, Page 63; Figure 3, Page 64. From The Home Point System: Token Reinforcement Procedures for Application by Parents of Children with Behavior Problems, *Journal of Applied Behavior Analysis*. Used by permission of the authors.

Exceptional Children. Figure 3, Page 35. From O'Leary and Becker, Behavior Modification of an Adjustment Class: A Token Reinforcement Program. Used by permission of the publisher.

Wahler, R. G. Figure 4, Page 66. From Oppositional Children: A Quest for Parental Reinforcement Control, *Journal of Applied Behavior Analysis*. Used by permission of the author and the publisher.

Research Press Company. Figure 1, Page 77. From Guide for Group Leaders for *Parents Are Teachers* by Wesley C. Becker. Used by permission of the publisher.

Holt, Rinehart and Winston. Pages 167–168. From A Learning Theory Approach to the Treatment of the School Phobic Child by Gerald R. Patterson in *Case Studies in Behavior Modification,* edited by Leonard P. Ullmann and Leonard Krasner. Copyright © 1965 by Holt, Rinehart and Winston, Inc. Reprinted by permission of Holt, Rinehart and Winston, Inc.

Index

Dr. Wesley Becker, who has his doctorate in psychology from Stanford University, has spent his professional career working with the needs of children and parents. He is the author of three books on children, parents, education, and psychology. He has also been the author or coauthor of numerous articles in parents' magazines, Sunday supplements, and professional journals.

Dr. Becker grew up in a family of ten children and now has thirty-eight nieces and nephews, a fact that helped lead him to his interest in children and parents. He is currently co-director of a Follow Through project in Oregon involving nearly 10,000 disadvantaged children.

Janis Becker received her bachelor's degree in psychology from the University of Illinois and is now working toward her master's degree in special education at the University of Oregon. She has been the coauthor of several articles on special education in professional journals.